50 EARLY MEDIEVAL FINDS
FROM THE PORTABLE ANTIQUITIES SCHEME

Jo Ahmet & Simon Maslin

AMBERLEY

First published 2024

Amberley Publishing
The Hill, Stroud
Gloucestershire, GL5 4EP

www.amberley-books.com

ISBN 978 1 3981 1891 1 (print)
ISBN 978 1 3981 1892 8 (ebook)

British Library Cataloguing in Publication Data.
A catalogue record for this book is available from the British Library.

Typeset in 10pt on 13pt Celeste.
Typesetting by SJmagic DESIGN SERVICES, India.
Printed in the UK.

Contents

Introduction

The centuries between the end of the Roman empire in Britain, *c.* AD 410, and the Norman Conquest in 1066 represent one of the most fascinating and complex periods of British history. Long written off as the mysterious 'Dark Ages' thanks to an archaeological record that was, compared with its Roman precedents, relatively obscure, this period holds a deep and enduring fascination. Today it is more commonly referred to as the 'Early Medieval' period, but it contains a diverse range of historical events and cultures that defy such a simple label. This era contains the foundations of what would define the later Middle Ages and succeeding eras; everything from language, law, churches, monasticism, patterns of land use, agriculture and our very social fabric has its formative origins here. This is the age of Anglo-Saxon and Viking, of Pict and Scot, the age of Offa, Alfred the Great, Eric Bloodaxe and Harald Hardrada. The stories, tropes and legends from this period are now ubiquitous cultural institutions, inspiring films, books, TV shows and video games. The daily lives of the people of the period, by contrast, remain far more opaque.

It wasn't until the nineteenth century that the distinct archaeology of this period really became recognised, largely thanks to a number of accidental discoveries of strikingly ornate groups of grave goods which seized the public imagination. Previously such objects had often been credited to the supposedly more culturally advanced Romans. Today the archaeology of the Early Medieval period is still somewhat diffuse, with settlements characterised by timber buildings which leave only the faintest traces in the ground. Meanwhile, the religious and royal institutions of this period have ambiguous archaeological footprints profoundly different to those we recognise from later periods and are consequently the source of endless debate and discussion. In fact, the majority of sites of the period have left us no visible remains above ground at all that can still be seen and little in the way of any monuments that can be visited. By contrast, it is the artefacts from the period that offer us the most spectacular glimpse of this world; the royal burials of Sutton Hoo, Prittlewell and Taplow, which have provided us with world-famous examples of the incredible richness of the artefacts, decorative arts of the age and skill of the craftspeople.

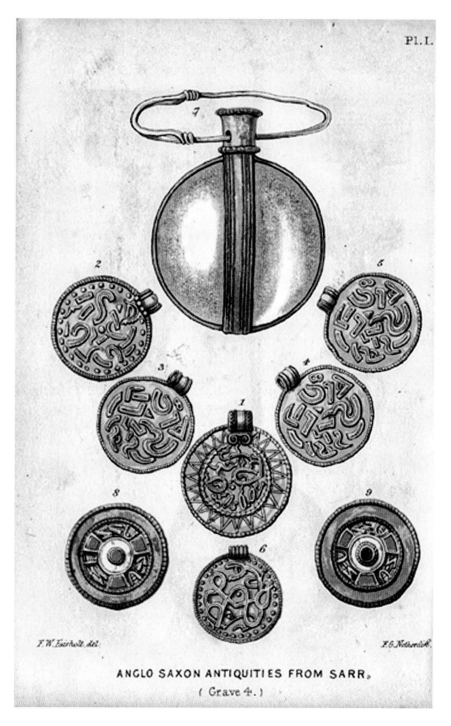

Pl. I.

ANGLO SAXON ANTIQUITIES FROM SARR,

(Grave 4.)

Images of necklace elements from a high-status woman's grave from Sarre, Kent. These are some of the first published illustrations of objects from the period after some of the first excavations of an Anglo-Saxon cemetery. (CO-0 1863. John Brent, *Account of the Society's Researches in the Saxon Cemetery at Sarr (sarre) Part 1*, Archaeologia Cantiana, Vol. 5 1863, Plate I)

A reconstruction of the Anglo-Saxon Great Hall complex at Lyminge, Kent, as it would have appeared in the later sixth to seventh centuries AD. This important royal estate centre, home to King Æthebert of Kent and later redeveloped as a Christian monastic site, demonstrates some of the key characteristics of settlement archaeology in this period with its collection of enigmatic sunken featured buildings and large and intricately constructed timber halls, which are now preserved only as faint traces in the soil. Settlement sites of this period often have very little in the way of associated metal artefacts. (© University of Reading, Mark Gridley)

The work of the Portable Antiquities Scheme (PAS) in the last twenty years has been fundamental in adding to these scattered images of the period, with a wide range of new objects being recorded from across the country on its database (accessible at www.finds. org.uk). By engaging with the general public and hobby detectorists across the nation to ensure that finds are properly recorded, we can open up the archaeological process to everyone, with immense contributions to knowledge and understanding being the result. Most of these objects are finds that would never be found or recorded by archaeologists under normal circumstances, often found far from known sites. At the time of writing, there are over 35,000 Early Medieval objects (not including coins) on the PAS database, with brooches, strap ends and pins representing the largest discrete groups. These to a certain degree represent the archaeological 'background noise' of items dropped and lost by people travelling and working in the landscape. Some also represent activities at unexcavated settlement and market sites as well as burials disturbed and scattered by the plough. Collectively they provide a huge amount of information about the dress, customs, histories and beliefs of the people who lived, worked, fought and died in this country in the latter half of the first millennium AD.

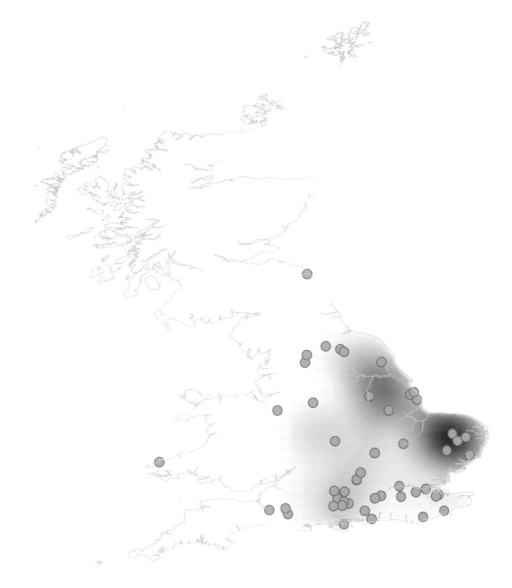

A map showing the locations of the fifty finds discussed in this book (green dots) overlaid on the overall density of objects found from the period (red shading). The largest number of individual finds from this period come from East Anglia and the eastern side of England. (Contains OS data, © Crown copyright OGL 2023)

The distribution of finds from this period across the country reflects a number of factors. Different areas and cultural groups produced different quantities and types of metalwork which means that some areas (such as Wales) produce relatively little in the way of locally distinctive finds whereas some areas (such as East Anglia) produce huge amounts. These patterns change with time and geography, creating a complex picture. On top of all of this is the additional fact that some areas see a lot of detecting activity and some don't, the

A gold mount from the Staffordshire Hoard (see Find 18), a dramatic and evocative example of an object from this period found by a detectorist. (WMID-0B5416, © The British Museum, licensed under CC BY-SA 4.0)

availability of land accessible for detecting playing a large part in determining how much gets recorded for different areas.

The aim of this book is to illustrate the breadth of these finds and the stories they tell by looking at fifty specific examples in more detail. The objects have been selected for a number of reasons; some comprise spectacular and rare high-status objects, some are just really good examples of humdrum everyday items which are found across the country. Many are also completely unique. We have mostly chosen to focus on individual objects over the (many) large and dramatic hoards known from the period to provide what we hope is a clearer picture of what the individual finds can tell us. All of these finds tell stories of the period and the historical and social changes of the time and all have been found by members of the public and recorded with the PAS. Their records remain accessible in the public domain as a virtual museum of fascinating and sometimes mysterious glimpses into the past.

Chapter 1
After Rome:
The Fifth to Sixth Centuries AD

The end of Roman authority in the province of Britannia is traditionally dated around AD 410 with the withdrawal of the province's remaining military forces to fight in Gaul, leaving the rest of the population to fend for themselves. This was an event that heralded monumental changes for the people of Britain, impacting almost every aspect of their world. It was not an instantaneous process, however, and the fifth century AD can be seen as a dynamic time of waning Roman political influence and a persistence of Romano-British culture in the face of profound new cultural transformations.

These changes were not consistent across the island. The peoples of lowland southern and eastern Britain quickly found themselves dealing with Germanic migration that

A reconstruction of Canterbury in the mid to late fifth century AD with Anglo-Saxon timber buildings and small-scale occupation present among the ruined and abandoned Roman buildings. (© Canterbury Museums & Galleries)

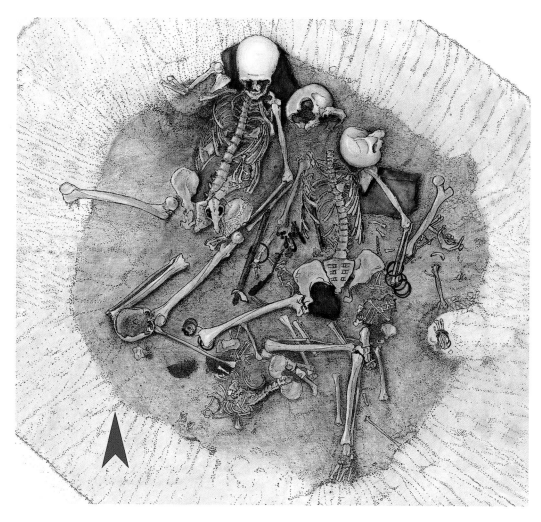

A triple burial from Beer Cart Lane, Canterbury. The individuals were interned with a mixture of late Roman-style metalwork and Germanic glass beads, showing the complex mix of cultural influences present in society at the time. (© Canterbury Archaeological Trust)

had, by now, been sweeping across western Europe for over a century. In contrast, life in Scotland and the Atlantic fringe experienced something of a cultural resurgence. The contrasting situations these areas found themselves in would come to define regional differences which, in some cases, exist to this day.

The archaeology of the fifth and sixth centuries AD demonstrates new styles of burial, artistic fashions and types of artefact, which reflect newly emerging elites and power structures. In many areas society transformed beyond recognition from a Christian Romano-British to a pagan and distinctly Anglo-Saxon culture. Ultimately this process would supplant the languages people spoke, the placenames they used and the genetic heritage of the population. This period also saw dazzling crafts and vibrant cultural modes spread across the land, changes that are strongly reflected in the range of metal-detector finds recorded by the Portable Antiquities Scheme.

Despite the collapse of Roman control in Britain at the beginning of the fifth century AD, Roman objects remained in use by some. This buckle plate is distinctly Roman in form. Its decoration is late Roman, consisting of a central palmette, a running bar design, punched rows of crescents and opposing animal heads. These elements are also, however, key features of the first distinctly Early Medieval art style, the quoit brooch style.

This was initially popular on objects associated with military dress, particularly buckles with which this object would likely have been paired. Even rarer finds, such as sword and scabbard fittings, also occur. Dating for these objects generally has them occurring from the second half of the fourth century and towards the end of the fifth century AD. Indeed, it appears that nearly half of the style's period of use was after the apparent end of Roman rule in AD 410.

The quoit brooch style is not restricted to Britain, with examples effectively straddling the English Channel, although concentrations are noted in Hampshire, the Isle of Wight and Kent. This geographic spread and clear connection with an elite trying to display a militaristic image may point towards the last vestiges of the Roman army and bureaucratic classes trying in vain to maintain cross-Channel connections.

A quoit brooch-style buckle, with its distinctive paired beast heads, running bar design and palmette. (WREX-AEACCA ©National Museum Wales, licensed under CC BY 2.0)

This square buckle from Kent is of a type frequently aligned with the quoit brooch style, and similar buckles may have been paired with the buckle plate discussed here. Of note is that the type occurs as late as the beginning of the sixth century in Anglo-Saxon graves like those at Highdown, Sussex. (KENT-79B261, © Kent County Council licensed under CC BY 4.0)

This rare scabbard chape fragment has the distinct palmette and running bar and animal designs seen on the proceeding objects. (SUR-029B13, © Surrey County Council licensed under CC BY2.0)

A striking feature of Early Medieval archaeology is inscribed objects, those using runes being perhaps most widely known. Ogham, an insular alphabet with a heartland around the Irish sea periphery, does, however, appear to predate the arrival of the Germanic runic alphabet in the British Isles. Ogham was used primarily to write forms of archaic Gaelic, although some examples in old Norse and Pictish have been suggested from Scotland. Its letters mostly consist of various lines emanating from a central line or seam, with the earliest examples having the seam aligned vertically and designed to be read bottom to top.

Ogham lends itself to monumental inscriptions, with the corner of upright stones functioning as the seam. This example imitates the form but in miniature, utilising a small, fine-grained sandstone bar in place of a monolith. The engraved lettering along the object's corners is almost identical to that on monumental stones, although its use on multiple corners is much scarcer. Portable examples such as this are incredibly rare, with barely a handful known: a cauldron from Kilgulbin East, County Kerry; a limestone spindle whorl from Buckquoy, Orkney; and a bone knife handle from south-west Norfolk. A recent translation of this object reads: MALDUMCAIL / S / LASS. The first part of the inscription contains the Gaelic name of an individual, Mael Dumcail. The second part, however, remains undeciphered. This find was generously donated to the Herbert Museum, Coventry, by the finder.

The Coventry miniature Ogham stone. (WMID-634A9A, © Birmingham Museums Trust licensed under CC BY 2.0)

The Ogham stone from the churchyard of Kilmalkedar, County Kerry, Ireland. This example shows the typical corner use for the inscription of many Ogham stones, in the format aped by the Coventry miniature stone. (Used under CC 0)

While the earliest quoit brooch-style objects are strikingly military in nature, the style gets its name from large silver annular 'quoit' brooches, on which the style was first recognised. These brooches, when found in archaeological contexts, occur in female graves from the middle of the fifth to early sixth century, many furnished in a distinctly Anglo-Saxon style.

It is clear that over the course of the fifth century the style was adopted beyond the military fittings on which it originated, most notably the female-gendered adornment such as these brooches. While these may be the most iconic, other types of adornment do occur, such as this decorated bracelet fragment. Despite being incomplete, the distinct decoration seen before – palmettes, running bars and C or S scrolls – is still clear.

While it is possible the longevity of this style after *c.* AD 410 may be linked to surviving Romano-British populations, its widening use on other objects may tell another story. Incoming Anglo-Saxon groups may have seen displays of Roman military power as something to aspire to and to add validity to their own status. With, as we shall see later, the huge amount of wealth displayed on Anglo-Saxon objects typically associated with women it may be that the this elite style was simply co-opted into incoming Anglo-Saxons' already established displays of elite status.

The Kent bracelet fragment, with its distinct decoration. (KENT-06B559, © Kent County Council licensed under CC BY 2.0)

A quoit brooch-style mount from Hampshire with red enamel to emphasise the design. This rare example of a non-military or female dress accessory shows many of the typical features of the style. (HAMP-FFCDF4, © Winchester Museums Service licensed under CC BY 2.0)

One of the most striking things about the arrival of the Anglo-Saxons is the plethora of new brooch types to arrive with the incoming settlers. One group of indigenous brooches, however, have something of a renaissance: the penannular type. The type is defined by having an almost annular frame with a narrow break in its circumference. This example has a frame that terminates in solid ribbed terminals, a common feature of the resurgent

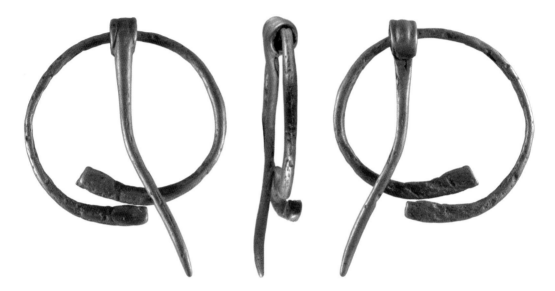

A penannular brooch of Booth's class F from Pembrokeshire. (NMGW-EBFCB6, © The Portable Antiquities Scheme licensed under CC BY 2.0)

A large silver and amber Pictish-style penannular brooch from Galway, Ireland, *c.* AD 900. (MET 1981.413, © Metropolitan Museum of Art licensed under CC0 1.0, with background edit by the authors)

16

The penannular-brooch sculpture by Alan Burke, outside the Saint Patrick Centre, Downpatrick, Ireland. A great example of the brooch type's influence on modern thought. (© Eric Jones licensed by CC BY-SA 2.0)

repertoire. Many of these Early Medieval penannular brooches also have a very distinct pin with ribbed loops which, unlike many other brooches, allow the pins to be easily identifiable when they've become detached.

These brooches have their origins way back in the Iron Age, surviving sporadically throughout the Roman period. Some subtypes, particularly a small, thick type with large square terminals, seem to have survived from the first century AD, although their heyday is in the sixth century. What is striking about these brooches is that they seem to be spread across both England and Wales, running counter to the often very regional spread of Anglo-Saxon brooches. From the eighth century, the type generally fell out of use in England and Wales, although they remained popular among the Picts in what is now Scotland and those areas controlled by Irish groups. The very late brooches, often in precious metals, are seldom found outside of Ireland, but are some of the most famed objects from the period. These striking silver and gold brooches would become symbols of the period in Ireland and since the nineteenth century AD have become a symbol of shared Celtic identity.

Of all the incoming new fashions to arrive with the Germanic settlers, the saucer brooch is one of the earliest, with some appearing as early as *c.* AD 430. These brooches are made from gilt copper alloy and have, as the name suggests, a saucer shape formed from a decorated circular face with raised angled rim.

The first examples to arrive follow similar forms as those in northern Germany and the Netherlands. They were made by applying a decorated stamped foil to a solid back and are known as applied saucer brooches. These are followed by cast one-piece examples. This example is one of the latter; its running spiral design following motifs common on the original applied examples, however, providing direct continuation between the two types.

From the second half of the fifth century, there is a great flowering in variety of the designs used on the saucer brooches, and even derivatives of the overall form. Notable new designs from this period include swastikas, stars and even the earliest forms of Anglo-Saxon-style animal art. There is also a notable increase in size over the course of their use, which is in contrast to one of their derivatives, the much smaller button brooch. By the middle of the sixth century the designs being used, and even the form, were very distinct from those used on the near Continent.

This type is mostly known from burial contexts in southern central England, where they occur in pairs. There is, however, a bit of a spread over time into neighbouring areas, particularly Kent and the Isle of Wight. The paired brooches are usually identical types and forms, with some showing evidence of repairs – perhaps in an attempt to keep a paired set. However, like their distribution, this changes over time, becoming more inconsistent by the time they fell out of use in the second half of the sixth century. Since the advent of the PAS and regular reporting of the type by metal detectorists, the general historic patterns are supported, although clusters are now known in East Anglia and recorded from as far north as Catterick.

Gilt copper-alloy saucer brooch from Hampshire. (HAMP-005BE3, © Winchester Museum Service licensed by CC BY-SA 4.0)

From above left: a lead die for making applied saucer brooch foils (see Find 11) (NMS-BC1EAC, © Norfolk County Council); a later Style I (see Find 9) saucer brooch with distinct interlace (WAW-3AA3C4, © Birmingham Museums Trust); a tiny button brooch with barely visible vertical rim (IOW-7F2C72, © Isle of Wight Council); a Frankish button brooch or miniature saucer brooch with vertical rims and central cell for now missing garnet, the latter feature rarely seen on Anglo-Saxon equivalents (KENT-4B2C25, © Kent County Council). All shown to a comparative scale displaying how relatively small the button brooches are. (All licensed by CC BY-SA 4.0)

A pair of very late saucer brooches combining the Salin I zoomorphic style and garnet inlay. Found during excavation near Prittlewell, Essex. This combination is highly unusual and can be seen as the culmination of the type under the influence of the latest design techniques of the second half of the sixth century AD. (© MOLA/Andy Chopping)

While coins are not the focus of this book (as they form a rather large topic of their own), their influence on Early Medieval material culture is undeniable. Some contemporary objects such as gold bracteate pendants clearly copy coin designs (see Find 11), others like this pendant incorporate coins directly into their very construction. Formed from a gold *tremissis* coin of the Byzantine Emperor Maurice Tiberius (582–602) with the simple addition of a plain gold suspension loop this coin is transformed from a piece of currency or bullion into an item of personal adornment.

Such pendants were highly popular in the later sixth and seventh centuries AD and heavily favoured the gold Roman style *tremissis* and the larger *solidus* coins still being produced by the Byzantine (eastern Roman) Empire. The coins themselves seemed to be imported widely into northern Europe and were increasingly copied by local rulers. Such imitations were not necessarily meant as forgeries but to convey legitimacy based on a widespread acceptance of the original type. These latter coins tend to be referred to as pseudo-imperial in that they copy the Byzantine issues imprecisely but to a sufficient degree where they are recognised as such. The coin utilised in this pendant is indeed one such copy, likely produced in Lombardic-controlled northern Italy.

Maurice Tiberius seems to have been a popular emperor to copy. While this may have simply been due to his long reign at the height of coin-pendant popularity, there may be a

A gold *tremissis* coin (*solidus* fraction popular in the seventh century) of Maurice Tiberius utilised as a pendant, found in Yorkshire, probably another pseudo-imperial issue. (YORYM-701955, © York Museums Trust licensed by CC BY-SA 2.0)

Above: Another gold coin of Maurice Tiberius, this time a *solidus* utilised as a pendant, found in Kent (KENT-AC7E52, © Kent County Council licensed by CC BY-SA 2.0). *Below*: A gold Frankish *tremissis* utilised as a pendant, found in Durham and likely slightly later than the above two, when the Byzantine connection is becoming less important and the names of northern European towns (in this case Huy in modern Belgium) and local notables become more important (DUR-EFD9E4, © Durham County Council licensed by CC BY-SA 2.0).

more direct influence. Maurice recruited a large number of Germanic mercenaries into his armies and while this certainly included Franks it may also have included Anglo-Saxons. If this was the case then direct interaction with the Byzantine state and society may account for the popularity of his coinage and perhaps even contributed to the noted increase of overtly Byzantine objects being deposited in graves from the beginning of the seventh century AD.

Chapter 2
The New Kingdoms:
The Sixth to Seventh Centuries AD

The growth of regional identities, centralised authority and kingship, alongside the process of Christian conversion, saw profound cultural changes overtake Britain during the sixth and seventh centuries AD. The growth of kingdoms sees the development of the group of polities known as the Heptarchy (rule of seven) – Northumbria, Mercia, Wessex, East Anglia and Kent along with Sussex and Essex – who vied for supremacy and power over the next few centuries. For the first time we also have real evidence from written sources

A reconstruction of an Anglo-Saxon long hall at Wychurst, Kent. Halls like these would have formed the centre of ruling estates throughout the landscape. (© Elaine Butler/Regia Anglorum)

Providing early material evidence of the politics of the emerging kingdoms, this gold *tremissis* (pale shilling) of Two Emperors type dating *c.* 650–70, found in Kent, may have been struck to demonstrate an early political alliance. (KENT-672C14, © Kent County Council licensed under CC BY 2.0)

about the individual rulers, with names to add to these histories. The Early Medieval Church established itself in England during this period following St Augustine's mission to Kent in AD 597. The centuries that follow see its rapid development with dual influences from distant Rome and the powerful Celtic Christian identity of Ireland and the western fringe of Britain.

These developments paralleled expansion in trade and connectivity across the North Sea and Channel, with new ideas, fashions and ways of living being introduced. This is the period when the first gold coins since the Roman period are struck, testifying to an increasing complexity of regional power and economy. Archaeologically, these changes manifest in new types of 'central place' settlements such as royal estates where wealth and authority were concentrated, as well as lavishly furnished burials, such as Taplow, Harpole, Prittlewell (see image on p. 24) and, of course, Sutton Hoo. This period produces some of the most iconic 'Anglo-Saxon' objects thanks to the prevailing fashion for gold and garnet jewellery and intricate gold filigree metalwork culminating in material like that found in the Staffordshire Hoard (Find 18), almost certainly the single most important archaeological find of the period made by a detectorist.

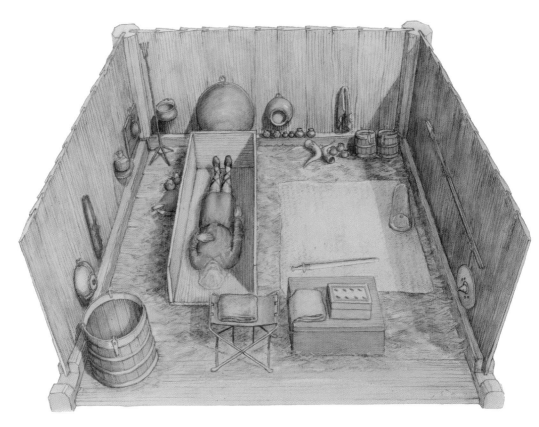

Richly furnished burials at sites such as Prittlewell provide us with a huge amount of evidence for a period where decorative metalwork and personal ornamentation were key indicators of wealth, status and power. (© MOLA/Faith Vardy)

7. Frankish zoomorphic and anthropomorphic scabbard chape, AD 400–600, Hampshire (HAMP-4CBF82)
Dimensions: 38.8 mm × 25.35 mm × 10.3 mm

During this period, the development of the emerging royal elites in southern England was influenced in many ways by their more established Frankish counterparts. The most significant result of these influences was the process of conversion to Christianity, first instigated in Kent by King Æthelberht and his Frankish Queen Bertha, which expanded rapidly across the country by the end of the seventh century. Evidence of Continental connections at a more day-to-day level can also be seen in the material culture, in the form of small finds that demonstrate Frankish styles, fashions and stylistic influences.

This striking anthropomorphic and zoomorphic object is a scabbard chape, of Frankish style, designed to protect and decorate the end of a sword scabbard. It depicts a male face, with round staring eyes, a wide mouth and a distinctive haircut, which is flanked by a curving pair of birds' heads, perhaps ravens or eagles. Below these is a narrow projecting body terminating in a rounded knop at the end of the scabbard. The rear has a hooked fitting with a rivet hole to secure the chape to the scabbard. Similar examples are found in France, Germany and Italy and seem to echo the pagan Germanic past that underpinned the various cultures of this era in north-western Europe, despite the Frankish kingdom being nominally Christian by this time.

Frankish zoomorphic and anthropomorphic scabbard chape, AD 400–600, Hampshire. (HAMP-4CBF82, © Winchester Museums Service licensed under CC BY-SA 4.0)

Another version showing the same basic elements, except here the upper portion takes the form of a stylised beast head, Hampshire. (BERK-9B9169, © Portable Antiquities Scheme licensed under CC BY 2.0)

Iron objects such as weapons and tools, despite being ubiquitous in daily life during this period, rarely survive to be reported by the PAS, having long since rusted away to nothing. Even when they do survive they are often overlooked and are difficult to identify or date with any confidence.

This find is a good example of a rare survivor of an iron object that is unambiguously of this period. It is a very distinctive type of throwing axe called a *francisca*, a weapon most famously used by the Franks but also widely used by other Germanic peoples including the Anglo-Saxons. The short haft and distinctive curved blade on this axe made it highly effective in close quarters, where it could be used to hook and pull down shields, but its main use was as a missile, being thrown en masse by a charging force of warriors with the intention of breaking the enemy line.

Iron axehead, AD 500–580, from Cambridgeshire. (CAM-5D8F2E, © Cambridgeshire County Council licensed under CC BY 2.0)

9. Gilded mount, AD 500–600, from Muchelney, Somerset (SOM-92E674)
Dimensions: 34.7 mm × 11.9 mm × 9.7 mm

This distinctive little rectangular object is made of gilded copper alloy and decorated with a deeply moulded zoomorphic motif framed by a heavy linear border. The interlaced ornament depicts an elongated beast, facing right, with a head with a circular eye, lines for jaws and a sinuous body with two curved limbs below. The design is rendered in what is called Salin Style I, a distinctive phase of Anglo-Saxon art beginning as far back as the later fifth century AD, which presents dense jumbles of animal and geometric forms rendered in a distinctive deeply incised and fragmented style.

The object is curved with integral fixing rivets and flared terminals at either end. The function is most likely decorative. The usual interpretation for mounts like this is that they were used to decorate straps on horse bridles. As with so many decorative objects from this period, however, there is considerable uncertainty about the way they were utilised and many other examples lack obvious fittings. The focus on sinuous animal forms seen on objects like this is perhaps the most characteristic element of pre-Christian Anglo-Saxon art and over the course of the next century developed through several stages to culminate in some of the most iconic artistic expressions of the age. This find was donated to the Somerset Museum Service.

Gilded mount, AD 500–600, from Somerset with Style I decoration; an interpretation of the animal in the design is shown on the right. (SOM-92E674, © Somerset County Council licensed under CC BY 2.0)

Gilded mounts from Hampshire (SUR-25B8CC, © Surrey County Council licensed under CC BY 2.0) and Buckinghamshire showing panels of Style I decoration (BUC-F6FE23 & BUC-215ED8, © Buckinghamshire County Museum licensed under CC BY-SA 4.0).

This brooch is a fine example of one of the most extravagant forms of early Anglo-Saxon dress accessory in the later fifth and sixth centuries AD: the great square-headed brooch. This particular example is visually stunning, with gilt 'chip-carved' ornament comprising panels of intricate Salin Style I decoration with geometric and zoomorphic motifs. In the corners of the head these panels frame small lenticular settings containing slab-cut garnets. There is another small circular setting for a small red gemstone on the bow. The foot has flanking beast heads projecting out in front of three large, rounded lobes which contain settings for more cut gemstones or glass inlays, now lost.

These large and dramatic forms of brooch along with equally elaborate cruciform brooches, were a powerful (if not tremendously practical) form of display among communities of this period, particularly in East Anglia where they are most frequently found. Although quintessentially 'Anglo-Saxon' cultural objects, they represent the pinnacle of a long tradition of Germanic brooch design, stretching back into the Roman period, with variations encountered across a wide range of Scandinavian and European areas. This tradition was very much emblematic of a world of tribal communities and chiefdoms, where personal displays of wealth and status were key aspects of community life, visually defining the place of the individual in the hierarchy of society.

Great square-headed brooch, AD 450–700, Milton Keynes. (BUC-F2BD87, © The Portable Antiquities Scheme licensed under CC BY 2.0)

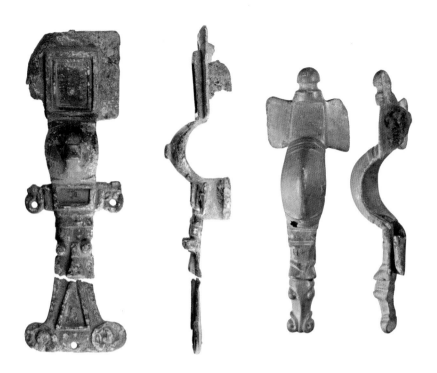

Cruciform brooches, AD 475–550, from Lincolnshire (DUR-65352E, © Durham County Council licensed under CC BY 2.0) and Yorkshire (NLM-692811, © North Lincolnshire Museum licensed under CC BY 2.0).

The style of these large, ornate and high-status brooches was imitated in smaller and more simply decorated types called 'small-long' brooches. These are relatively common finds from the period AD 450–550, Lincolnshire (LIN-EAA01C, © The Portable Antiquities Scheme licensed under CC BY 2.0) and Northamptonshire (NARC-11ECC8, © Northamptonshire County Council licensed under CC BY-SA 4.0).

Thin decorative metal appliqué plaques, often in gold, were key elements of the decorative design of dress accessories, weapons and war gear from the Anglo-Saxon period. These plaques were made using the Pressblech technique, whereby thin precious metal foil was pressed onto a die stamp to force the design into the metal. While the products of this technique can be seen on a wide range of items (see Find 5), the dies themselves are rare finds.

This unusual example of a Pressblech die is circular, flat and decorated on the front and plain on the back. It depicts a heavily stylised figure with large, bulbous eyes atop a triangular chin/beard with large lips. The arms are parallel to the body until the elbows, which bend outwards at 90 degrees. Each hand is holding a snake. The figure is wearing a belt made up of pellets. The legs are in a crouched position and are bent at the knees. The torso is facing forward while the legs are facing to the right.

What makes this find particularly remarkable is the fact that the design is matched exactly to that of a gold bracteate pendant found at the Riseley cemetery site in Kent, which was excavated in 1937–38 by the Dartford District Antiquarian Society. This find, one of four gold pendants from the site, is now in the Dartford Borough Museum. It is extremely unusual to be able to match a die to its finished products in this way, especially given the distance between the findspots, which in turn demonstrates the wide-ranging contacts of the makers and wearers of these designs. It also adds to the increasing evidence that these spectacular objects were being produced in England as well as Scandinavia where they have long been seen as originating from.

Pressblech die, AD 600–700, from Thatcham, West Berkshire (BERK-34B1CA, © Portable Antiquities Scheme licensed under CC BY 2.0); on the right is the bracteate pendant from Riseley, Dartford (image © Dartford Borough Museum).

From top left: an incomplete *Pressblech* die stamp from Canterbury, Kent, which was likely used in the production of disc or saucer brooches (Find 5) (HAMP-BB2D18, © Portable Antiquities Scheme); an example from the Isle of Wight, which made foil appliqués decorated in Style I (see Find 9) (IOW-E6AEA9, c Portable Antiquities Scheme); an unusual example depicting a face similar to that used for button brooches, Buckinghamshire (SUR-073AC0, © Surrey County Council); a rectangular stamp from Staffordshire with interlace similar to Style II, which may have decorated objects similar to those from the Staffordshire Hoard (Find 18) (LIN-490483, © Portable Antiquities Scheme). Here the animal's eye can be seen top right from which descend the pitch-fork jaws. (All licensed under CC BY 2.0)

This iron spearhead has a characteristic conical split shaft and lozenge-shaped tapering blade which immediately marks it out as being of Early Medieval date. Many similar examples are known from burial contexts dating to the sixth and seventh centuries AD. The blade has been purposefully bent into a curve, presumably before deposition in the course of the River Wey near Woking in Surrey. This suggests a deliberate 'killing' and sacrifice of what would have been an expensive weapon. It is part of a wider pattern from pre-Christian England where finds of weapons in watercourses and marshy places have been recorded – were these offerings to the gods? Some sort of appeasement? Or perhaps a plea for good fortune in battle?

Above left: A deliberately bent iron spearhead, AD 550–650, Surrey. (SUR-0EC561, © Surrey County Council licensed under CC BY 2.0)

Above right: Another riverbed find – this one is intact and hasn't been bent. From Lincolnshire. (LIN-2939BF, © Portable Antiquities Scheme licensed under CC BY 2.0)

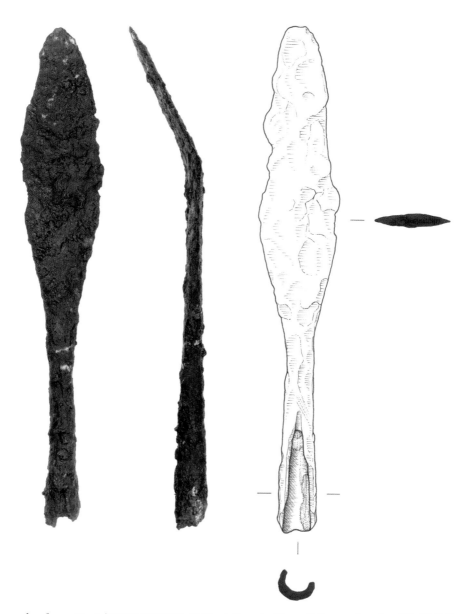

Examples from Kent (KENT-0B9AD2, © Kent County Council licensed under CC BY 2.0) and Suffolk (SF-44FC96, © Suffolk County Council licensed under CC BY 2.0). Spearheads like this are most commonly found in furnished inhumation burials of this period.

While we lack understanding of the finer details of such practices, objects like this give us direct indications about the existence of pagan communities, sometimes (as here) in areas where little other occupation evidence is known. This particular find, recovered by magnet fishing from the present-day river channel, is paralleled by several other examples recorded in pre-PAS days from the sites of silted up paleochannels in the wider area and clearly forms only part of a broader pattern of deposition. It was donated by the finder to Guildford Museum, Surrey.

13. A figurine depicting a man, AD 600–650, West Berkshire (BERK-0929C9)
Dimensions: 51.2 mm × 13.1 mm × 6.6 mm

This cast copper-alloy figurine of a male is posed apparently naked, gesturing with hands held out at the waist and with his thumbs projecting up. The face has a pointed chin, which may suggest a beard, and the features are simple to the point of abstraction, as is characteristic for depictions of human faces during this period. There are two rounded projections at the sides of the head which may be part of a headdress or just his ears.

This unusual figure is paralleled by a small number of other examples found on the eastern side of the country, including a female figurine from Kent now in the British Museum (BM 1988,0412.1) and a number from East Anglia, some of which are illustrated here.

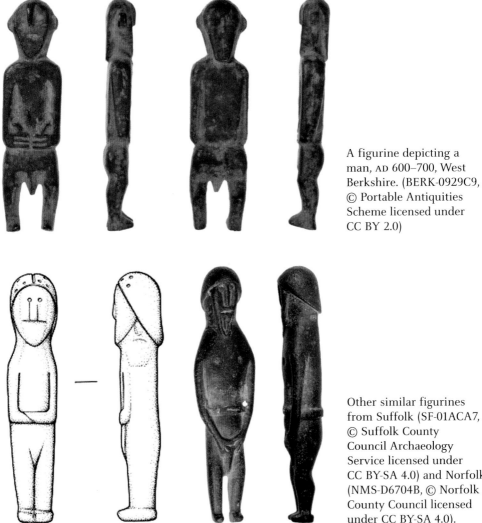

A figurine depicting a man, AD 600–700, West Berkshire. (BERK-0929C9, © Portable Antiquities Scheme licensed under CC BY 2.0)

Other similar figurines from Suffolk (SF-01ACA7, © Suffolk County Council Archaeology Service licensed under CC BY-SA 4.0) and Norfolk (NMS-D6704B, © Norfolk County Council licensed under CC BY-SA 4.0).

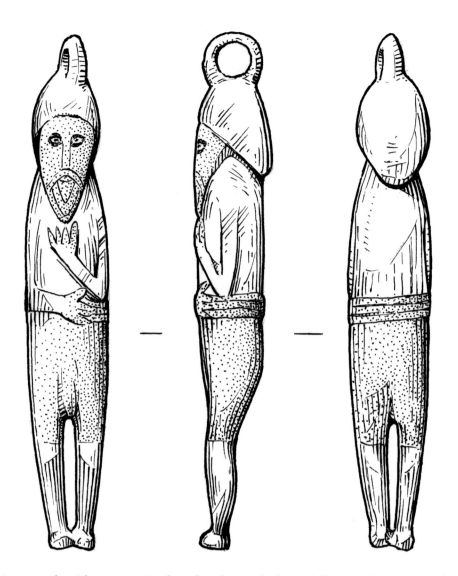

An example with a suspension loop found near the later sixth–seventh-century Anglo-Saxon settlement and cemetery site of Carlton Coleville, Suffolk. (© Portable Antiquities Scheme licensed under CC BY-SA 4.0)

Similar objects are known from across Scandinavia and the pre-Christian Continent. This example would appear to blend elements from those overseas examples with more local influences. It vividly demonstrates the connection between pre-conversion Germanic cultures in England at this time and the wider pagan traditions of the Germanic world.

As to who the figure represents, a likely explanation is a god or mythical character, perhaps the pagan Anglo-Saxon equivalent of Frey, the Norse god of fertility. It may have had an intended amuletic or votive function, but as with many other material aspects of pre-Christian tradition, we have no real understanding of what it represented to whoever owned it.

This extraordinary gilded copper-alloy mount depicts a staring horned human face with eyes set with red stones (either garnets or coloured glass) above a long, drooping moustache and triangular beard. The hair is uncovered and has two curved horns projecting, one to either side, which meet above the head with a pair of bird or serpent head terminals.

Images of faces with horn-helmeted figures as well as whole figures, often in pairs and sometimes performing ceremonial dances with weapons, are known from objects produced in Germanic cultural areas dating from the seventh century AD until the early Viking period. They are generally thought to be a representation of the chief Anglo-Saxon god Woden (the Norse Odin) and are perhaps some of the most direct expressions of pre-Christian Germanic religion that we see in decorative metalwork from this period. Famous examples from Britain can be seen on the Sutton Hoo helmet and the Finglesham buckle. There are many other examples known from across the Scandinavian and Germanic Iron Age and Early Medieval periods. Such was the pervasive influence of the identity of Woden that he is frequently cited as being more than a god – and is recorded as being the ancestor of many early Anglo-Saxon ruling dynasties in England.

Images like this on small items of personal adornment and dress are often the best tangible evidence that we have of the survival of pagan ideas and iconography into the middle of the seventh century AD. They provide rare and fascinating insights into a changing world and are always important to record.

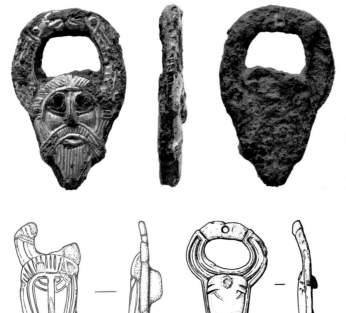

Anthropomorphic mount, AD 600–700, from Kings Worthy, Hampshire. (BERK-DB4E15, © Portable Antiquities Scheme licensed under CC BY 2.0)

A similar example from Essex (SF-F9D919, © Suffolk County Council licensed under CC BY 2.0) and another from Norfolk (NMS-F90626, © Norfolk County Council) showing mounting rivets on the reverse.

This dazzling gold and garnet object is a buckle plate, part of a set of decorative elements from the belt of a high-status individual of the seventh century AD. The plate consists of a gold backing plate, originally folded around a (now missing) buckle frame and held together with gold rivets. The front of the plate is richly decorated with gold and garnet cloisonné cell-work, comprising cells made of thin strips of vertically aligned sheet gold that hold slab-cut garnets backed by cross-hatched foils. These foil backings are designed to catch the light, enhancing the sparkle of the stones, garnet being far less lustrous than other gems. Around the outside of this panel of garnets runs a border of beaded gold wire or 'filigree'.

The technique of decorating fine objects with garnets was introduced from the Continent in the early sixth century AD. It flourished first in Kent before spreading around much of early Anglo-Saxon England before reaching a culmination of quality and intricacy during

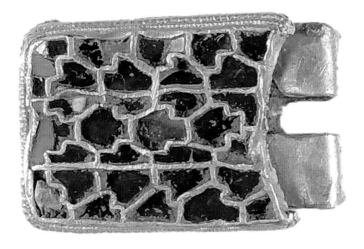

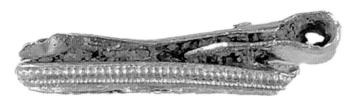

Gold and garnet belt buckle, AD 575–700, Lincolnshire. (LIN-B6F0ED, © Portable Antiquities Scheme licensed under CC BY 2.0)

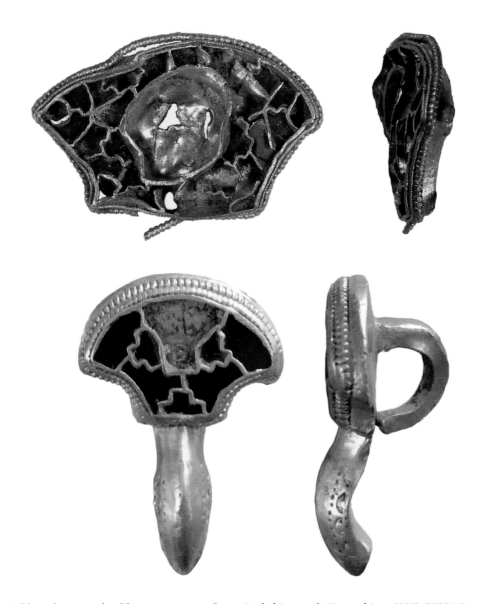

Gold and garnet buckle components from Berkshire and Hampshire. (SUR-E72BAE and SUR-920F4E, © Surrey County Council licensed under CC BY 2.0)

the seventh century AD exemplified by objects such as the shoulder clasps from Sutton Hoo in Suffolk. It required incredible skill, by craftspeople working without magnification aids and has proved difficult to replicate even with modern tools.

The buckle plate appears to have been intentionally separated from its frame, suggesting it may have been modified for reuse as a decorative dress accessory or even as bullion. This pattern of removal and reuse of expensive goldwork is seen in other finds such as the Staffordshire Hoard (Find 18) and shows us that such objects could often be subject to a long lifespan of adaptation and modification.

The seventh century AD saw a rapid expansion of Christianity among the population of lowland England, with missions from Rome and Ireland creating a diverse tapestry of faith in the population. One of the most tangible indicators of this process are the new forms of material expression that begin to be made and worn. This is most visible in material associated with high-status members of society and perhaps most dramatically in the form of gem-set gold pectoral equal-armed crosses. The most famous example of one of these items is probably that recovered from the late seventh-century tomb of St Cuthbert in Durham cathedral.

Gold pectoral cross pendant, AD 600–700, Norfolk. (NMS-6E94EA, © Portable Antiquities Scheme licensed under CC BY 2.0)

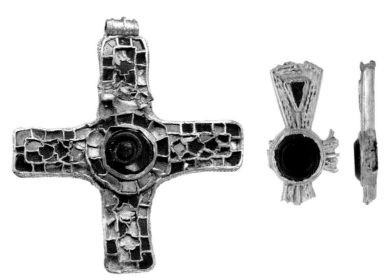

Gold and cloisonné garnet pendant from Yorkshire (YORYM214, © Portable Antiquities Scheme licensed under CC BY-SA 4.0) and a gold filigree and garnet example from Kent (KENT-9D33EB, © Kent County Council licensed under CC BY 2.0).

41

A different manifestation of the same basic cruciform motif, this time on a gold filigree disc pendant, AD 600–700, Rutland. (LEIC-47932A, © Leicestershire County Council licensed under CC BY 2.0)

In recent years a number of other examples have come to light, found in professional excavations of furnished burials as well as stray finds by metal detectorists, most likely from ploughed-out burials. These are a diverse group of objects in their form and construction, variously constructed using gold filigree, cabochon gems, or cloisonné garnets held in sheet-gold settings. It is likely that they were either worn singly or as part of more elaborate collars or necklaces, with spacer beads, disc pendants and smaller garnet pendants (Find 17). It is notable that when found in graves these usually appear to have been buried with women. The example found with St Cuthbert is therefore perhaps unusual in being associated with a man, as is another found with the supposedly 'masculine' assemblage of the Staffordshire Hoard (Find 18).

The example shown here is incomplete as is typical for such a fragile item recovered from churned-up ploughsoil. It comprises three of the original four arms and the suspension loop, richly decorated with gold wire filigree which frames sheet-gold collets at the centre and the ends of the arms which hold cabochon garnet stones. While not as elaborate as some other examples, it would have been an expensive item and was no doubt worn by some senior authority of the period. The find was reported under the 1996 Treasure Act and has been acquired by Norwich Castle Museum.

17. Gold and garnet pendant, AD 600–700, Norfolk (NMS-B1F206)
Dimensions: 17.4 mm × 14.5 mm × 2.5 mm

This gold oval pendant has a cabochon red garnet surrounded by an outer border of twelve radially set cloisonné cells inlaid with foil-backed garnets. It was most likely part of a composite necklace or collar, strung with gold beads, coin pendants (Find 6), *bullae* and perhaps with a central gold cross or disc pendant at the centre (Find 16). This is most clearly seen in examples from eastern England, particularly Harpole and Desborough (Northamptonshire), the latter now in the British Museum (British Museum 1876,0504.1).

These lavish displays of wealth would have been very high-status items, perhaps even used as religious or secular badges of office. So lavish were these objects that they are

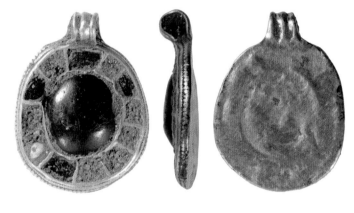

Gold and garnet pendant, AD 600–700, Norfolk. (NMS-B1F206, © Norfolk County Council licensed under CC BY-SA 4.0)

Rectangular and triangular examples from Gloucestershire (GLO-9C3FFD, © Bristol City Council licensed under CC BY 2.0) and Suffolk (SF-40EE34, © Suffolk County Council licensed under CC BY-SA 4.0); other examples holding pieces of reused Roman millefiori glass from Oxfordshire (OXON-AE2CF9, © Oxfordshire County Council licensed under CC BY 2.0) and Yorkshire (YORYM-74E44A, © York Museums Trust licensed under CC BY 2.0).

A gold and garnet disc pendant from Yorkshire. (LVPL-68E714, © National Museums Liverpool licensed under CC BY-SA 4.0)

A reconstructed necklace of the period featuring pendants (see Find 17), spacer beads and a pectoral cross (see Find 16). (© Lloyd Bosworth 2023)

alluded to by Christian writers in the succeeding century, such as the Venerable Bede, when extolling women to be more reserved in their appearance.

The increase in metal-detecting over the last few decades has dramatically increased the number of objects like this which are known. Most are typically simpler than this example, but can be square, rectangular, circular, oval or triangular depending on the shape of the stone, which is typically held in a simple filigree frame, soldered to a sheet-gold backing plate with a single suspension loop at the top. The item is here pictured 'as found' with compacted soil remaining in some of the settings. Cleaning and conserving composite items like this requires expert intervention and when in doubt the best advice is to leave it well alone.

Without doubt the single most important find from the Early Medieval period to have ever been made by a detectorist is the Staffordshire Hoard. Comprising almost 6 kg of fragmentary gold and silver fittings, this incredible group is a dramatic example of the intricacies of Anglo-Saxon art as well as a snapshot of the power dynamics of the seventh century AD. This was a time of continuous conflict, fluctuating borders and endemic violence, when powerful warlords displayed their wealth in the form of intricate goldwork on their weapons and dress. This goldwork incorporates cloisonné cell-work and filigree to create decorative motifs combining elements of the emergent Christian religion used alongside older cultural associations. Many elements are fine examples of Salin Style II, the quintessential visual language of the period, characterised by animals with interlaced bodies and distinctive jaws and eye settings.

The items in the hoard mainly comprise sword fittings, many clearly ripped from their attachments and intentionally damaged. Alongside these are pieces of other forms of war gear such as helmets and horse-harness fittings. Perhaps more surprising is that it contained some overtly Christian religious objects such as processional crosses directly linked to religious practices. The hoard was recovered from ploughsoil, apparently having been scattered by agricultural activity. Excavation of the site did not demonstrate any clearly associated structures or features. With this context of isolation and the nature and treatment of the hoard contents, the interpretation is one of a group looted bullion, perhaps from a battle, deliberately buried at some point between AD 650 and 675, in an age of upheaval and uncertainty.

A selection of items from the Staffordshire Hoard. (© Birmingham Museums Trust)

Chapter 3

Hegemony and High Kings: The Seventh to Mid-Ninth Centuries AD

The later seventh and eighth centuries saw a period of incessant warfare between the kingdoms of the Heptarchy, with different regional polities attaining dominance; first Kent, then Northumbria, then Mercia and finally Wessex. This is the age of Offa of Mercia, the first Anglo-Saxon ruler whose power and influence was truly international, and who was recognised in Frankia and Rome. More broadly, this is also what has long been known as the 'Middle' Anglo-Saxon period, a time of profound economic, political and religious development as the myriad smaller Saxon and British polities of England were absorbed by the major powers of the day, leaving four kingdoms: Mercia, Wessex, East Anglia and Northumbria.

This period sees the emergence of a distinctive class of religious and economic centres known as minsters, which flourished during a golden age of early monasticism. These early religious centres were hubs for crafts and responsible for the production of many of the objects we find from this period. The Venerable Bede, who lived and worked in one of these monastic communities at this time, also provides us with the first and most influential history of the age. Here too are *wics*, important trading hubs that drove growth and political unions across the seas. Archaeologically, this period sees the end of furnished inhumations and thus the removal of a critical body of material evidence from the record. Luckily, a vast corpus of finds recorded with PAS has helped to fill in some of these gaps in knowledge.

The end of this period is a time of massive upheaval, with the first incursions of a people who would profoundly change life in Britain – the Vikings. This would effectively bring an end to the early monastic developments and also to the independence of the English kingdoms.

Offa of Mercia depicted on a coin of AD 765–92 found in Kent. (KENT-60B28C, © Kent County Council licensed under CC BY 2.0)

This collection of copper-alloy fragments is all that remains of a very rare type of Early Medieval artefact known as a 'hanging bowl'. These were high-status items, often lavishly decorated with enamel and precious-metal inlays, and were likely valuable and prized objects which served as a focus for communal events such as feasts. The functional origins of these vessels lie in the Roman period, but by this time they were being manufactured in the western (Celtic) areas of the British Isles and appear to have become desirable items in

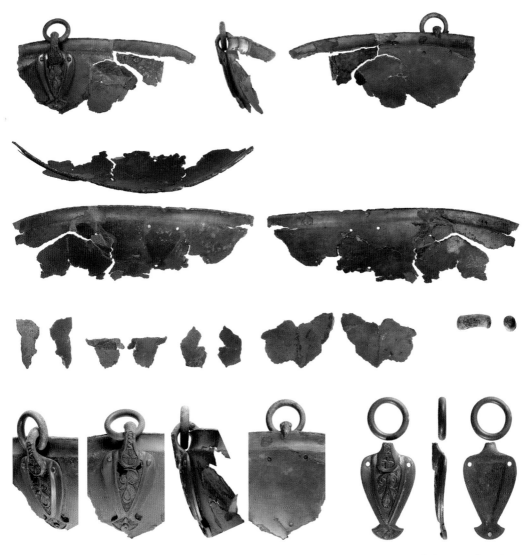

A hanging bowl, AD 500–700, Yorkshire. (SWYOR-9C315A, © West Yorkshire Archaeology Advisory Service licensed under CC BY 2.0)

Two hanging-bowl suspension escutcheons found separate from their bowls: a large zoomorphic example with enamelled interlace, Wiltshire (SUR-BFDCEE, © Surrey County Council licensed under CC BY 2.0) and a small example with simple geometric decoration, Kent (KENT-78BC77, © Kent County Council licensed under CC BY 2.0).

Anglo-Saxon cultural areas to the east. Their precise function is, however, unclear, as with so many other aspects of life at this time.

This find is fragmentary and includes part of the rim, which would originally have had a diameter of around 200 mm, along with fragments of sheet metal from the body of the bowl and two of the escutcheons with their suspension loops. These escutcheons are both zoomorphic, modelled in the form of birds with wings folded back and fine, red enamel champlevé decoration on the back. The heads and beaks form the hooks at the top which hold the rings; these originally would have been attached to a suspension chain allowing the bowl to be hung.

While the more robust suspension mounts are sometimes found by detectorists, a complete or near complete example such as this is very unusual. Typically, finding something like this would be good evidence for a disturbed burial, with these objects often recovered during archaeological excavations of seventh-century graves. This example was acquired by Skipton Museum.

This extraordinary gold object is a double-sided bezel from a gold signet ring of Frankish type. Originally designed to pivot on an axis bar running between the shoulders of the (now lost) hoop, it has engraved designs on both sides, either of which could be pressed into wax to make an impression. One side depicts a long-haired facing bust with a cross above and stylized drapery below, with a retrograde legend around which reads 'BALdEhILDIS' (Balthild). The other side depicts a male and a long-haired female figure embracing beneath a cross. The attribution to a female name on such a high-status object is very unusual. The scene on the reverse is perhaps suggestive of betrothal, which may suggest a role for this object.

This type of swivel ring is known from a few rare Continental examples dating to the seventh century. However, examples from the Anglo-Saxon world are not known. The Frankish form of the name Baldhild is not a particularly rare name as far as we know, nor is its Anglo-Saxon equivalent Bealdhild. This particular name however does present a tantalising possible historical connection to an Anglo-Saxon woman who married Frankish King Clovis II around AD 648, and who acted as queen regent after his death in AD 657.

This object, along with other contemporary examples of gold jewellery, demonstrates the overseas connections of the English elite. The mixtures of Continental and Anglo-Saxon motifs with both pagan and Christian symbolism all evoke the wider world of this period. In many cases, such objects comprise isolated and accidental losses and are unlikely to be found through any method other than metal-detecting.

A gold signet ring of
Frankish type named to
Balthild, AD 600–700, Norfolk.
(PAS-8709C3, © The British
Museum licensed under
CC BY-SA 4.0)

Another Frankish signet ring,
this one with interlace (Style II)
decoration on the hoop and a
bezel depicting a figure holding
a cross and a bird with another
bird above, AD 580–650, Essex.
(ESS-E396B1, © Colchester and
Ipswich Museum Service licensed
under CC BY-SA 4.0)

This small, triangular buckle plate is decorated with lavish champlevé enamel. It shows a triskele motif flanked by a pair of beasts in profile with jaws agape, appearing to bite a circular setting at the narrow end for a missing stone or enamel boss. At the wide end are two fixing points, surrounded with panels of decoration comprising enamel with glass insets.

The decoration of this object is very distinctive and of a style paralleled by examples from Ireland dating to the seventh or eighth centuries AD. This type of distinctively Irish metalwork represents an uncommon type of find in England and Wales; but where it does occur, it points to overseas connections for the local population. Was this object brought back to the Danelaw as the spoils of raiders? Or was it the possession of a trader or other traveller who dropped it? Whatever the precise origin, it demonstrates how interconnected the lands of the British Isles and Ireland were during this period, when the sea provided the easiest transportation route for trade, conquest and the spread of new ideas.

Left: Buckle plate decorated with Irish-style enamelling, AD 600–900, Lincolnshire. (LIN-89F702, © Portable Antiquities Scheme licensed under CC BY 2.0)

Below: Buckles of Irish style from Wiltshire (WILT-41265C, © Salisbury and South Wiltshire Museum licensed under CC BY 2.0) and Warwickshire (WMID-6E662D, © Birmingham Museums Trust licensed under CC BY 2.0).

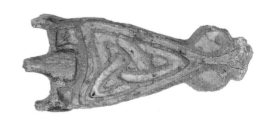

This small circular plaque or mount has an expanding-armed cross of retained metal inlaid with champlevé enamel inset with small squares of millefiori glass. This ancient technique of glass-making uses bundles of fused rods of different colours which are then cut into slices to create patterned inserts. Here the decoration alternates red and white squares at the end of each arm with black and white chequered squares at the centre and in the quarters between the arms. The surrounding enamel has faded so its original colour is uncertain.

This type of enamel and millefiori decoration has a long history of use in Irish metalwork and this disc was most likely soldered to a larger item as part of its decoration. Similar forms of decoration can be seen on famous finds from the period such as the Oseberg bucket, which demonstrate artistic connections between the Irish, English and Scandinavian worlds. A likely explanation for the presence of this little mount in Dorset is that it perhaps represents a component of a similar item, perhaps a reliquary or casket, and is part of the lost or discarded spoils of a Viking raid.

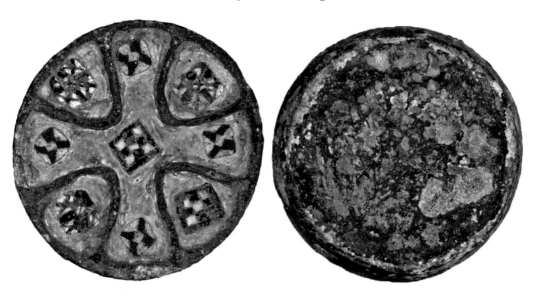

An enamel and millefiori mount, AD 670–900, Dorset. (DOR-E48B7B, © Somerset County Council licensed under CC BY 2.0)

This dramatic-looking object is a decorative terminal, probably from a drinking horn, modelled in the form of a fearsome beast's head, posed with ears back, eyes wide and jaws agape. The features incorporate cells inlaid with enamel and there are traces of gilding on the surface demonstrating that this would have been a finely decorated object. The open ends of the jaws are connected with an integrally cast bar; this likely secured a ring, chain or other attachment intended for suspension. The head emerges from a conical body that is decorated with interlace and a pair of spiral motifs running in a band around the open end, which has rivet holes for securing it to the horn.

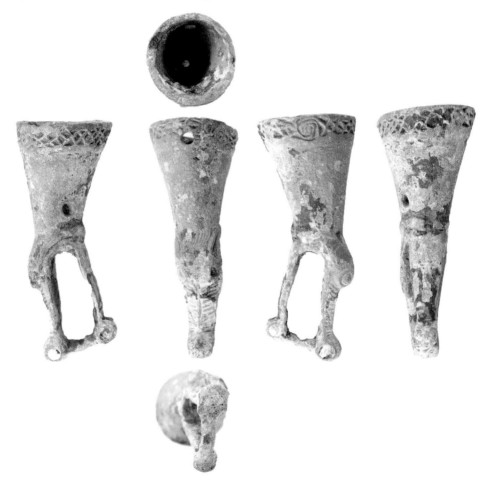

A zoomorphic terminal, probably from a drinking horn, AD 700–800, Thames foreshore, London. (LON-EFCF31, © Museum of London licensed under CC BY-SA 4.0)

While other objects suspected to be drinking-horn terminals are known, this one is particularly unusual in having enamel inlay, which is a feature more widely seen in Irish metalwork and suggests that it was made abroad. An expensive and likely exotic high-status decoration, it represents the culture of communal feasting which lay at the very centre of the lives of the elite. Such feasts would see kings and their retinues gathering in large timber halls to drink, tell stories, distribute largesse, broker power and forge alliances; activities recounted to us most famously in the epic poem *Beowulf*.

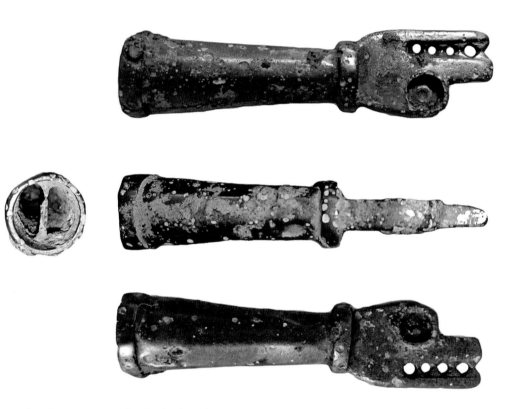

Another rare example of a drinking-horn terminal, this time with a much simpler head featuring inlaid eyes, Leicestershire. (DENO-55E157, © Derby Museums Trust licensed under CC BY 2.0)

24. A glass mount, possibly from a reliquary or bowl, AD 750–900, Lincolnshire (LIN-C31CD7)
Dimensions: 23 mm × 17.5 mm

Discovering glass from this period is exceptionally unusual, not least because it is fragile and can't be found using a metal detector! A rare survivor, this conical bi-chrome glass stud alternates opaque grey and deep-blue semi-opaque glass, worked in a feathered pattern. The object is core formed, with the glass being wrapped/trailed or slumped around a clay core, a technique seldom seen outside of bead manufacture since the first century AD. The colours have likely dulled due to weathering but would have been vibrant when new. Glasswork like this became very fashionable in the later eighth century as Irish insular traditions began to be widely imitated by English monastic workshops in the production and decoration of high-status products of various kinds.

As to what it was for, this unusual item was possibly used alone as a gaming piece but perhaps more likely mounted in a metal cell as a cabochon setting to decorate a large object like a vessel, reliquary, processional cross or book cover. At this time glass was a rare and precious material, used as a substitute for gems and examples of glass cabochons mounted on fine silver vessels are known from the Witham hanging bowl (sadly now lost) and inside the Ormside bowl. We can date this particular piece on its own merits both by the style of the glass working and the general form. There will, however, always be some ambiguities in precisely determining how such a decorative item like this would have actually been used.

Above left: A glass mount, possibly from a reliquary or bowl, AD 750–900, Lincolnshire. (LIN-C31CD7, © Lincolnshire County Council licensed under CC BY-SA 4.0)

Above right: A similar object made with twisted strands of glass, perhaps also used as a mount inset or from an item of personal dress such as an amulet, Lincolnshire. (LIN-252D32, © Lincolnshire County Council licensed under CC BY-SA 4.0)

25. Runic silver strap end, AD 800–850, Hampshire (SUR-4A9C55)
Dimensions: 41.1 mm × 10.9 mm × 2.4 mm.

Strap ends are among the most common Early Medieval stray finds. Typically, they have zoomorphic terminals in the form of beast heads and a range of decoration. Dating to the eighth to eleventh centuries, they functioned as belt or strap terminals for both men and women, and may also have adorned harnesses, sword belts and other types of straps. What makes this particular example unusual is that it was cast with an inscription on both sides in old English runes. The inscription on this example reads: *'œiereleworo / ogtœpis.œsil'* or *'Hemele wrohte þis gesil'*.

The particular significance of this inscription is the presence of the previously unrecorded Old English word *gesil*, which can be literally interpreted as 'strap end', the inscription thus translating as 'Hemele made this strap-end'. It is certainly uncommon for an archaeological find to add an entirely new word to Old English, which makes this object particularly special. It was reported under the 1996 Treasure Act and is now part of the collections of the Winchester City Museum.

A small number of other personal objects with runic inscriptions are also known from this period, most commonly these inscriptions comprise the owner's name or, as in this case, the maker. These finds give us a personal connection to the original owners, as well as tantalising clues about contemporary language, dialect and the use of the runic alphabet.

Above left: Runic silver strap end with the maker's name in runes, AD 800–925, Hampshire. (SUR-4A9C55, © Surrey County Council licensed under CC BY 2.0)

Above middle: A silver strap end with a female owner's name (*þ[-]œflœd*) scratched onto it, AD 800–925, West Sussex. (SUR-219F9A, © Surrey County Council licensed under CC BY 2.0)

Above right: A base metal object, possibly the handle from a spoon or other utensil which has been inscribed with a personal name, possibly read as either Byrnferþ, Biornferþ or Beornferþ, AD 700–1000, Norfolk. (NMS-2DC05C, © Norfolk County Council licensed under CC BY-SA 4.0)

This simple gold cross pendant is inscribed on one side with an inscription of six runes which read ᛖᚪᛞᚱᚢᚠ (eadr͡uf), most likely a personal name, perhaps of the owner. The form of the name seen here is very unusual and not recorded elsewhere, although it may perhaps represent a contracted or cryptic form of a more typical name such as Eardwulf. The inscription is flanked with a simple incised cross at the centre of each of the three surrounding arms, perhaps to reinforce the devotional message of the object. It is pierced for suspension at the base of the shaft which implies that it would be worn hanging downwards, which is an unusual aspect not seen on crosses worn in later periods.

This object represents a very early manifestation of personal Christian devotion, incorporating some distinctly pre-Christian elements, namely the runic lettering and the orientation of the cross. This orientation echoes the arrangement of pagan Thor's hammer amulets, known across the Germanic and Norse world. It may suggest to us that the wearer was part of a community very familiar with the wearing and use of such symbols, perhaps more so than the wider norms of the incoming Christian iconography.

This item was acquired by Berwick Museum and Art Gallery after having been reported under the 1996 Treasure Act.

 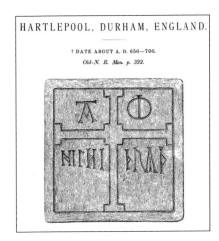

HARTLEPOOL, DURHAM, ENGLAND.

? DATE ABOUT A. D. 650—700.

Old-N. R. Mon. p. 392.

Above left: A gold cross pendant with runic inscription, AD 700–900, Northumberland. (DUR-B62F57, © Durham County Council licensed under CC BY 2.0)

Above right: A runestone from Hartlepool found in 1833 and dating to the later seventh century AD. Likely a Christian grave marker for a woman named as 'HILDITHRttH', it also incorporates the Greek alpha and omega (the beginning and the end). Runes like this were typically carved into hard materials such as stone or wood, their stiff angular forms being easier to scratch or cut into a surface than the curved Latin characters derived from the Roman world. Their adaptation for use on metalwork and small personal items hints at a much wider pattern of use on domestic objects and structures long since lost. (CO-0 1884. George Stephens, *Handbook of the old-northern runic monuments of Scandinavia and England*)

27. A silver-gilt disc brooch inscribed with a maker's name, Oxfordshire, AD 800–920 (OXON-2A467C)
Dimensions: 44 × 35.9 × 3.7 mm

This crumpled and incomplete silver-gilt disc is the front part of a disc brooch of a composite type. It was originally riveted to a copper-alloy backing plate, with which it was found. The brooch has decoration in the form of a cross made from interlaced floral, or knotted patterns along each arm of the cross which are gilded against the silver field. Within the border of the cross is an inscription in a script known as Anglo-Saxon Capitals, the most common form of lettering used in inscriptions between AD 700 and 1200. Compared with runic inscriptions, these have much more clearly recognisable origins in Roman lettering. It reads: + Æ L F G E [O] [-] M E A H [.] A H [.] H which can be read as '+ Ælfge- owns me...', the incomplete owner's name possibly being Elfgeard, Ælfgeat or Ælfgyfu. This text was inscribed during the manufacture of the brooch suggesting the item was specially commissioned for an important individual.

The use of a thin facing of precious metal on a cheaper base-metal backing plate, allowed production of an item which looked far more expensive than it actually was. It is a technique with its origins in post-Roman and Germanic brooches from 400 years earlier, when thin gold facings were applied to disc brooches (see Find 5). The delicate nature of the individual elements when separated has meant that complete or even fragmentary survivals are quite rare, even more so with inscriptions.

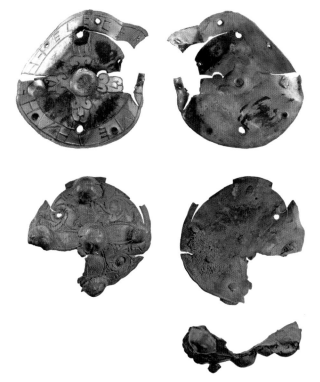

A silver-gilt disc brooch inscribed with a maker's name, Oxfordshire, AD 800–920. (OXON-2A467C, © Portable Antiquities Scheme licensed under CC BY 2.0)

Another example of a composite silver-gilt disc with floral decoration and domed rivet covers, Staffordshire, AD 800–1000. (WMID-614C9E, © Birmingham Museums Trust licensed under CC BY 2.0)

This little object, also known generically as a 'hooked tag' was an all-purpose fastener of simple design used to secure small bags or purses as well as clothing. It is triangular with a sharp hook at one end and attachment holes at the other to sew onto cloth or leather. Many of these objects are found by metal detectorists and they represent one of the more common everyday finds from the period.

This example is rather more elaborate than most. The plate is flat and features an engraved motif, which perhaps may be interpreted as leaves flanking a stem. The style of the design, with its sinuous forms rendered in high contrast against a background infilled with black niello (silver sulphide), was heavily influenced by contemporary manuscript illustrations and is known as the Trewhiddle style after the metalwork hoard from Cornwall dating to the late ninth century which exemplified it. Characteristically this style of decoration, often seen on silver items, incorporates several panels of lively decoration involving animals, plants and geometric forms. It became almost ubiquitous in England during the ninth century AD.

A silver hooked tag or clothing fastener, AD 800–900, Kent. (KENT-45B0A3, © Portable Antiquities Scheme licensed under CC BY 2.0)

Other hooked tags with zoomorphic forms in Trewhiddle style, Hampshire (SUR-19BC54, © Surrey County Council licensed under CC BY 2.0) and Northamptonshire (BH-340AB6, © Portable Antiquities Scheme licensed under CC BY 2.0).

This magnificent cast silver openwork disc brooch also boasts Trewhiddle decoration, enhanced with niello and features intricate openwork elements. It represents the pinnacle of this fashionable style in the later ninth century. The basic design is cruciform with two lozenge arm crosses, with concave sides and offset at 45 degrees and five large domed bosses. The terminals of each arm bifurcate into eight sinuous zoomorphic forms which fill the space within the cross panels. Unlike the composite brooch (Find 27) this is made from solid silver.

An openwork silver disc brooch decorated in the Trewhiddle style, Cheshire. (LVPL-590EDA, © National Museums Liverpool licensed under CC BY-SA 4.0)

Other elements of the hoard, including a coin which, crucially, provides a date for the entire assemblage. (© National Museums Liverpool licensed under CC BY-SA 4.0)

This brooch was found together with two other incomplete examples and a range of other finds including a coin of Wiglaf, King of Mercia, dated 830–840 AD. The inclusion of a coin in this group provides a good date for the items within it; typically detecting finds lack this crucial contextual information, so this is a particularly important find for dating both the Trewhiddle style and this type of brooch.

A number of other examples of these highly elaborate Anglo-Saxon brooches are known, each having a different variation on this basic cruciform arrangement dividing and bordering panels containing complex groups of interlaced plants and animals. Although mainly found in the eastern part of the country, a very similar example to this one, from Wales, may suggest localised Viking activity in the north-western part of Britain.

Later versions of the style, such as is seen on the Fuller brooch in the British Museum, introduce imagery connected with allegorical and biblical themes. Given the high-quality workmanship and the evident expense involved, these brooches must have been prestigious items and seem to have been highly fashionable among wealthy and high-status individuals in England at the time of Alfred the Great.

A comparable example from Wales. (LVPL-30A793, © National Museums Liverpool licensed under CC BY-SA 4.0)

30. A gold ring depicting the Agnus Dei, AD 800–900, Somerset (SOMDOR-46E1A1)
Dimensions: 26.52 mm × 14.11 mm × 9.06 mm

This gold ring is a rare and high-status personal piece of Christian symbolism. It has a large round bezel depicting the Agnus Dei (Lamb of God), standing left and looking backwards. The head of the lamb has a halo with notches which, when filled with niello as they would originally have been, would have presented the image of a cross. To the left of the animal there is a motif, probably representing the palm of Victory. The image has elements of the prevalent Trewhiddle style, so dominant at this time.

Other rings with this theme are known from this period – a few of which can be directly associated with named individuals, such as the ring of Alhstan, ninth-century bishop of Sherborne, now in the Victoria and Albert Museum and a ring named to Queen Æthelwith, now in the British Museum. The ring was declared Treasure under the 1996 Treasure Act and has been acquired by the Somerset County Museum, Taunton.

Right: A gold ring depicting the Agnus Dei, AD 800–900, Somerset. (SOMDOR-46E1A1, © Somerset Council and South West Heritage Trust licensed under CC BY-SA 4.0 and modified by the authors)

Below: A contemporary gold ring, *c*. AD 800–925, with zoomorphic Trewhiddle style decoration showing the continuation of earlier themes alongside the Christian motifs becoming increasingly prevalent during this period, North Yorkshire. (YORYM-EA5D0E, © York Museums Trust licensed under CC BY 2.0)

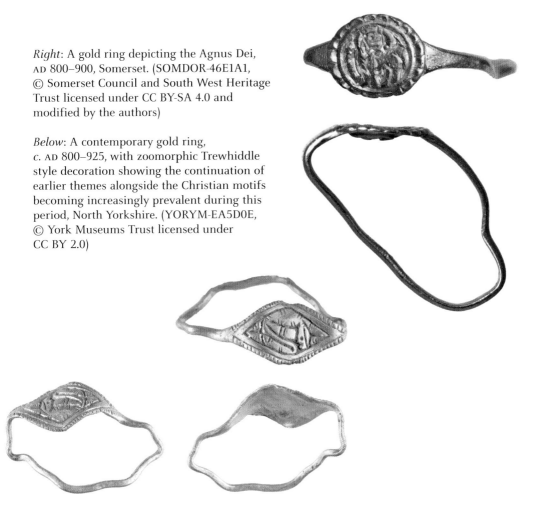

The growth in power of the Franks and the coalescence of the Holy Roman Empire under Charlemagne (AD 747–814) resulted in a Carolingian empire which dominated western and central Europe in the ninth century. This was to have a huge influence on the development of middle-Saxon politics and fashions throughout this period and well into the tenth century.

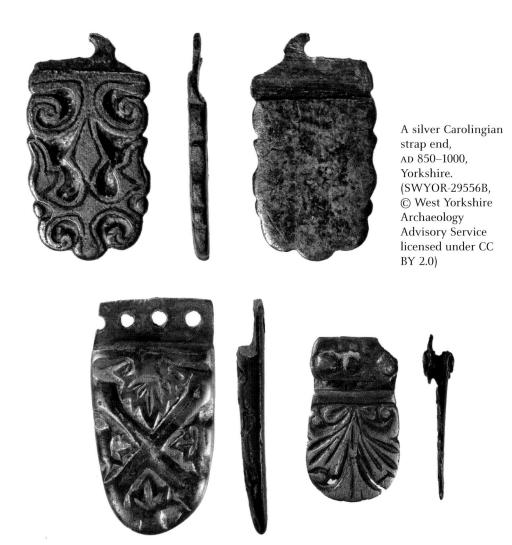

A silver Carolingian strap end, AD 850–1000, Yorkshire. (SWYOR-29556B, © West Yorkshire Archaeology Advisory Service licensed under CC BY 2.0)

Another silver strap end with acanthus-leaf decoration typical of the Carolingian type, Norfolk (NMS-55FBD7, © Portable Antiquities Scheme licensed under CC BY 2.0) and a silver strap end of Winchester style, displaying Carolingian influences, West Sussex (SUSS-0ED31C, © Portable Antiquities Scheme licensed under CC BY 2.0).

A number of high-status imported Continental objects are known from this era, identifiable from their characteristically stylised foliate ornamentation, which contrasts strongly with the prevalent naturalistic and zoomorphic styles of the Anglo-Saxon world.

This silver strap end is of typical 'Carolingian' form, being tongue-shaped with a symmetrical foliate design cast in high relief, the details emphasised by niello and gilding. The design features flanking scrolled leaves and scrolls emerging from a central stem, its base at the attachment end, which has a recessed flange (now incomplete) to rivet it to the strap. It is a distinctive expression of an identity that is quite different to that of local communities and was possibly worn by somebody either from the Continent or who wanted to demonstrate their Continental connections. The find was reported under the 1996 Treasure Act and has now been acquired by Yorkshire Museum.

Such striking styles from the Frankish world resulted in a proliferation of insular imitations, particularly in the areas of south-eastern England close to the Continent. In time these forms would be filtered through local metalworking traditions to become major influences on the tenth-century Anglo-Saxon art style known as the Winchester School.

An incomplete and slightly later silver-gilt strap end of Winchester style, AD 1000–50, Oxfordshire (SUR-970F39, © Surrey County Council licensed under CC BY-SA 4.0). The reverse depicts an Agnus Dei with a partial Old English inscription in Anglo-Saxon capitals reading -ð mec ah ('-ð owns me).

Chapter 4

Saxons, Danes and Vikings: The Mid-Ninth to Eleventh Centuries AD

From the later ninth century AD one story alone dominates the history of Britain, Vikings!, as is richly documented by the greatest history of the age, the *Anglo-Saxon Chronicle*. With the coalescence of Viking raids into an invasion by a 'great army' in the 880s, many aspects of life for ordinary people would have changed profoundly. This is the period of Alfred the Great, whose forces would preserve the independence of the last unconquered English kingdom, Wessex, and ultimately impose a truce with the invaders. Following this treaty was partition, with Danes laying claim to most of the north and eastern areas, establishing 'Danelaw'. New populations of Scandinavian settlers followed, with profound and far-reaching impact on the culture as well as the very language used in large areas of the country. Today this change, which affected some areas far more than others, is reflected in placenames and the varieties of archaeological finds recorded by the PAS, which are often very regionally specific.

The story of the eventual unification of the country under the West Saxon rulers Alfred, Edward and Æthelstan is now a fundamental part of our national narrative. As a process, it wasn't always straightforward, and by the early eleventh century AD the country had a Danish king and sat within an Anglo-Danish North Sea empire. An explosion in Anglo-Scandinavian styles and fashions, seen in objects from across this period and recorded by the PAS, allow us to map aspects of this process and get beyond the endlessly interrogated textual sources covering this most dramatic period of history.

A coin of Cnut dating to AD 1024–30, from Shropshire. (WMID-900DEE, © Birmingham Museums Trust licensed under CC BY 2.0)

The Anglo-Saxon world was one fundamentally built on wood, with buildings, ships and the utensils of everyday life all mostly crafted from this most versatile of materials. Consequently, so much of what they made has been lost to us from centuries of organic decay. Occasionally the tools used to create these things survive, however, and provide rare clues as to woodworking technologies and techniques.

This distinctive T-shaped axe is a characteristic tool of the Early Medieval carpenter. It has a gently curving blade and a large socket for a sturdy handle. The wide, narrow cutting edge made the tool light and highly versatile, and it could be used for a wide range of carpentry tasks; from cutting to shaving, planing and trimming. In the hands of a skilled craftsman, it could produce a flat, smooth surface to provide a high-quality finish for timber objects, vessels and structures. Being made of iron it is also a rare survivor, but it is directly comparable with excavated examples known from settlement sites. The most well-known examples come from a tool hoard recovered from the middle Saxon settlement at Flixborough, Lincolnshire.

Right: A woodworking axe, AD 700-1100, Yorkshire. (SWYOR-93AC56, © West Yorkshire Archaeology Advisory Service licensed under CC BY 2.0)

Below: A more iconic form of axe from this period, likely of Viking origin. This style of axe, in contrast to Find 32, was most probably a weapon, AD 800–1000, Wiltshire. (WILT-D49496, © Salisbury and South Wiltshire Museum licensed under CC BY 2.0)

This iron sword is of a type used by Viking raiders, although we cannot say for certain who actually carried this example, the type having been made and used in both Germanic and Scandinavian areas of north-western Europe. Found by magnet fishing within a watercourse, the sword is heavily corroded and the blade is badly damaged. The waterlogged depositional conditions preserve what may be traces of a grip made from wood or other organic material, but other fittings, such as a pommel, have been lost.

While copper-alloy and precious-metal fittings from swords of this period are not infrequently recorded, whole swords like this are exceptionally rare, and when found are usually only recovered, as with this example, from waterlogged contexts. An expensive item when new, its discovery invites the question of whether it was deliberately cast into the water as part of a pagan offering or just lost following a skirmish. Both explanations are possible given the history of the period, but we can never know for sure.

A Viking-style iron sword, AD 850–1050, East Sussex. (SUSS-959F28, © Sussex Archaeological Society licensed under CC BY 2.0)

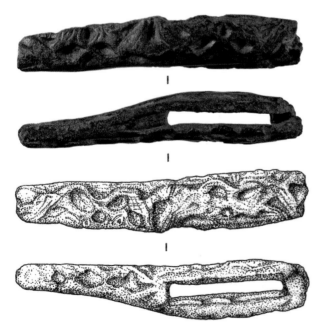

Swords like this were high-status items and would have been elaborately decorated to show off their wielder's power and prestige. This contemporary Scandinavian-style cross guard from a sword, also from East Sussex, gives a hint at the finely wrought detailing such weapons would have had. (SUSS-A0F30E, © Sussex Archaeological Society licensed under CC BY 2.0)

This finely made object, made from sheet gold and richly decorated with gold filigree, is one of a small but growing group of similar high-status terminal fittings. Some have been interpreted as being from *œstels* (pointers used to follow lines of text when reading from books) but they could also be terminals for silk laces attached to clothing. Whatever their function they were expensive and prestigious objects. This example, found by a detectorist in Suffolk, is hollow, with a domed terminal decorated with a concave-sided square frame with filigree scrollwork on the outside and a field of pellets within, all surrounding a small central setting for a blue cabochon glass stone.

These terminals come in a range of sizes; many are globular, like this example, but some are also made in the form of animal heads. All share distinctive features such as flat rear surfaces, perhaps to allow the object to rest on a surface or slide across a page, and a socket. This may have been for a shaft or a pointer made from an organic material such as ivory, or perhaps held a lace or cord attaching the object to something else. There is a suggestion of an integral hierarchy being represented within this group of objects, with higher-status examples using more exotic materials such as rock crystal and cabochon gemstones. The most famous and spectacular example of all is the Alfred Jewel (see image on p. 68), now in the Ashmolean Museum.

During this period, the rapid expansion of the Church created a powerful body of clergy with an increasing demand for religious books (see Find 42) and the various liturgical accessories used in services. It is certainly possible that objects like this could be seen in the context of the vestments, trappings and ceremonial activities of the ecclesiastical elite. As with so many finds from this period, however, there is a huge amount of mystery and uncertainty surrounding their purpose.

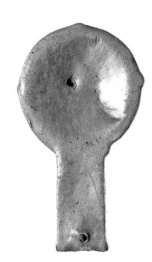

A gold and filigree terminal, perhaps from an *œstel*, AD 850–900, Suffolk. (SF-3ABEB9, © Suffolk County Council licensed under CC BY-SA 4.0)

Other examples of similar terminals from North Yorkshire (SWYOR-69C958, © West Yorkshire Archaeology Advisory Service licensed under CC BY-SA 4.0) and Northamptonshire (NARC-49D06E, © Northamptonshire County Council licensed under CC BY-SA 4.0).

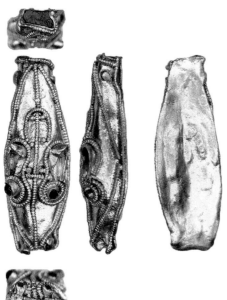

A zoomorphic example from Leicestershire. (LEIC-57BE78, © Leicestershire County Council licensed under CC BY 2.0)

The most famous example of one of these elaborate and enigmatic terminals, the late ninth-century Alfred Jewel, which has a figurative enamel and rock-crystal centrepiece surrounded by the lettering 'ÆLFRED MEC HEHT GEWYRCAN', or 'Alfred ordered me made'. (CO-0 1843, Henry Shaw, *Dresses and Decoration of the Middle Ages*, Vol. I)

This copper-alloy disc brooch is decorated with a very distinctive concave-sided quatrelobed motif in the Scandinavian Borre style, with four corners each extended to form interlaced, double-strand knots. It is a relatively common tenth-century type in East Anglia, found in areas where the population was either settlers from Scandinavia or heavily influenced by the fashions and customs of people from those areas. This particular example was one of two found relatively close together, suggesting perhaps that such brooches were worn in pairs.

Objects like this illustrate the rapid cultural change that occurred in the eastern parts of the country following the establishment of the Danelaw in the late ninth century, with new styles of metalwork becoming widespread. Variations in the style of the fittings used on these objects when compared to Scandinavian examples suggests that many, if not most, of these brooches were actually locally made by people who were clearly influenced by Scandinavian fashions but who may not themselves have originated from those areas.

An Anglo-Scandinavian disc brooch with Borre-style decoration, AD 900–1000, Norfolk. (NMS-E12321, © Norfolk County Council licensed under CC BY-SA 4.0)

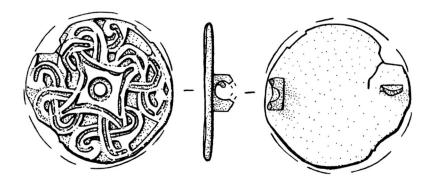

An illustration of an Anglo-Scandinavian disc brooch more clearly showing the spiralling interlace characteristic of the Borre style, Norfolk. (NMS-C65692, © Andrew Williams licensed under CC BY-SA 4.0)

36. A 'Viking'-style gold finger ring, AD 900–1100, Surrey (SUR-C33FB2)
Dimensions: 24.65 mm × 4.33 mm

This ring, although found in southern England, is of a type that is recognisably 'Viking' (or more correctly 'Scandinavian') and dates to the tenth or eleventh centuries AD. The wearer was perhaps either Danish or a local buying into the fashion for this style of jewellery, which had expanded across the North Sea area along with the Danish armies and their accompanying settlement in the Danelaw areas at the end of the ninth century AD. Items of personal dress and adornment produced in Britain began to be influenced by these new styles, a process that expanded far beyond the initial areas of contact.

The ring is composed of two plain circular-sectioned rods twisted together with two finer beaded wires which are twisted in between, resulting in alternating plain and beaded bands. The rods taper in diameter towards their ends which are hammered together to form a flattened join. The join is expanded and bears a decoration of four annular stamps. This particular example is gold and quite a substantial statement of wealth; however, the design was also copied in copper alloy and worn by less wealthy individuals.

A 'Viking'-style gold finger ring, AD 900–1100, Surrey. (SUR-C33FB2, © Surrey County Council licensed under CC BY 2.0)

A gilded copper-alloy example made in close imitation of a gold original, Wiltshire. (SUR-F97954, © Surrey County Council licensed under CC BY 2.0)

37. A hacksilver ingot cut from an arm ring, AD 900–1050, North Yorkshire (DUR-DFF172)
Dimensions: 24.8 mm × 9.3 mm

During the ninth to eleventh centuries AD the economy of the Danelaw was fundamentally based on silver bullion, with a transactional value derived from the weight of the metal, rather than the nature of the object itself. Viking raids and trade consequently distributed coins, jewellery and ingots as well as fragments of silver cut down to specific units of weight, generically called hacksilver, with small pieces used in daily transactions alongside or in place of standardised coinages.

This particular hacksilver ingot has a distinctive octagonal cross-section and punched annulet decoration, suggesting that it was originally part of an armlet of Hiberno-Viking type. It weighs 13.7 g which corresponds to around half of an *eyrir*, a Viking ounce (*c.* 26.6 g). Other ingots recorded by the PAS are far less diagnostic as to origin with many comprising simple hammered rods and bars which, when found in isolation, can be much more difficult to date.

A large number of comparable ingots have been found in hoards, along with coins and complete artefacts which better allow understanding of the dating and origins. Sometimes these hoards contain identifiable objects from across a truly huge area; from Ireland in the west, to Continental Europe, Scandinavia, Russia and all the way to the Middle East. Such hoards have been found across the British Isles, demonstrating the thriving and far-reaching trading and raiding economy of the time.

A hacksilver ingot cut from an arm ring, AD 900–1050, North Yorkshire. (DUR-DFF172, © Durham County Council licensed under CC BY 2.0)

The Silverdale Hoard (LANCUM-65C1B4): coins, hacksilver, whole armlets and silver ingots all found within a lead container. (© The British Museum licensed under CC BY-SA 4.0)

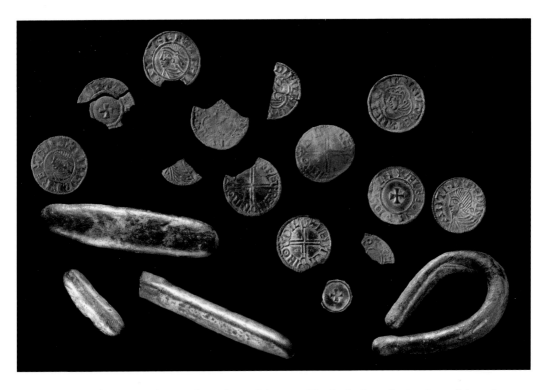

A small hoard of ingots and coins from the Welsh coast. The inclusion of coins in such hoards gives us excellent dating evidence both for the use of bullion in this form and also for the specific deposition date of this group. (NMGW-038729, © National Museum Wales licensed under CC BY 2.0)

38. A stitched leather shoe, *c.* AD 942–96, Kent (KENT-1122CD)
Dimensions: 230 mm × 95.37 mm × 31.72 mm

The rarest of all finds from the Early Medieval period are those made of perishable organic materials, most especially those which comprise elements of costume. This shoe is one such rare example, found preserved in anoxic waterlogged river sediments. It comprises a single piece of leather folded over the foot (referred to as a 'foot bag' type) or gathered as 'wrap around type' and stitched together with an integrated sole and upper. There is a double row of stitching at the top edge of the waisted midpoint with some thread remaining. Other areas have evidence of stitching, but this is less clear because of the condition of the shoe. Although it has lost some of its shape, the form of the toe suggests that it is for a right foot.

This shoe is unusual, and its construction is unclear due to its condition. It may have been gathered over the toe and instep with the seams indicating both sides were joined. Some evidence of possible repair is shown by the double seam. Although it most resembles shoes surviving from the Bronze Age, its double 'vented' back above the heel would point to a Roman or later date, although these are rare in Britain outside of Scotland after the sixth century AD. Following a period of public fundraising, a calibrated carbon-14 dating of *c.* AD 969 ± 27 was obtained which suggests that this example has a date range of AD 942–96.

A stitched leather shoe, *c.* AD 942–96, Kent. (KENT-1122CD, © Kent County Council licensed under CC BY 2.0)

In the early eleventh century AD, after many years of conflict, England was finally conquered by Danish rulers; first Swein Forkbeard and then his son Cnut, who ruled from AD 1016 to 1035. During this period the country became part of a North Sea empire, and Scandinavian art styles and fashions from this wider area became dominant influences. These were to have a profound effect on the vibrant insular Anglo-Scandinavian metalworking tradition that already existed in parts of the country (see Finds 35 and 36) and was now fast becoming the preferred fashion of the elite.

An Anglo-Scandinavian stirrup-strap mount, AD 1000–1100, Oxfordshire. (SUR-579E4D, © Surrey County Council licensed under CC BY 2.0)

Two examples of other forms of these very distinctive objects from Hampshire. (SUR-197F5C and SUR-000B25, © Surrey County Council licensed under CC BY 2.0)

A range of finds from this period vividly reflect these changes, perhaps most commonly elements of horse harnesses carrying designs influenced by the Scandinavian Ringerike and Urnes art traditions, of which this stirrup-strap mount is a particularly fine example. Designed to secure and protect the leather strap that held the stirrup, it was both a functional and a highly decorative object. Its front depicts a symmetrical pair of moulded interlaced beasts shown in profile and in high relief, with tendrils running from the backs of the heads to form flanking knops at the top of the plate and intertwined bodies which frame the rivet holes used to attach the mount to the strap and the stirrup iron. What is also interesting about this particular example is the additional engraved decoration on the reverse comprising the head of another beast with eye and lip lappet pointing towards the top. The purpose of this element of the decoration is unclear since it would have been concealed when in use.

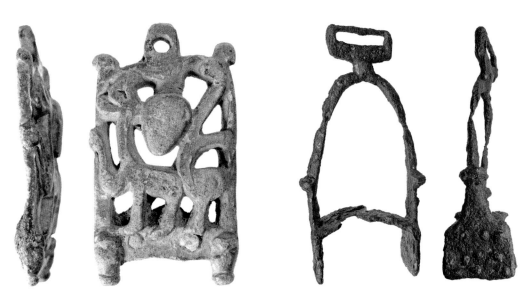

Above left: This unusual openwork example from Lincolnshire depicts a four-legged animal with one raised front paw and a curved tail over its back. It is a Continental import paralleled by examples from Denmark and Sweden. (SWYOR-37E516, © West Yorkshire Archaeology Advisory Service licensed under CC BY 2.0)

Above right: A contemporary iron stirrup showing the horizontal strap bar at the top to which these mounts would have been attached. From Warwickshire. (WAW-989551, © Birmingham Museums Trust licensed under CC BY-SA 4.0)

This incomplete copper-alloy object is one of a pair of functional and decorative bridle cheek-piece elements mounted on either end of an iron bit. These served to connect the straps of the bridle and reins to the bit, allowing the rider to control their mount. One strap loop remains, along with one of originally two flanking projecting zoomorphic terminals; this has a long neck which curls around to end in a head with jaws agape, biting its neck and with a distinctive tendril crest. At the base of the neck is an incomplete loop for the end of the bit, across which the item has broken, most likely due to wear and tear from long use.

The distinctive form and imagery derives from the Scandinavian Ringerike style. It would likely have been used in conjunction with strap fittings and stirrup-strap mounts of similar style (Find 39) as part of a distinctive suite of horse gear which is characteristic of this period (see reconstruction image on p. 77).

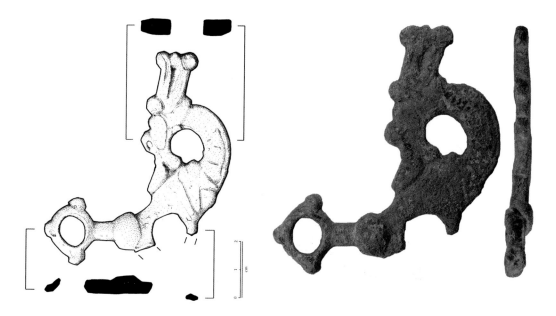

An Anglo-Scandinavian bridle bit cheek piece, AD 1000–1100, Kent. (SUSS-2D5753, © Sussex Archaeological Society licensed under CC BY-SA 4.0)

An Anglo-Scandinavian stirrup terminal decorated showing the same form of curved beast derived from the Ringerike style. These would have been used together with the bridle fittings and stirrup-strap mounts (Find 39) as part of matching sets of ornamented harness fittings which would have been highly decorative. Oxfordshire. (SUR-FD462E, © Surrey County Council licensed under CC BY 2.0)

A reconstructed eleventh-century horse and rider showing the location and use of the very distinctive items of Anglo-Scandinavian harness metalwork sometimes found by detectorists. (© Dominic Andrews)

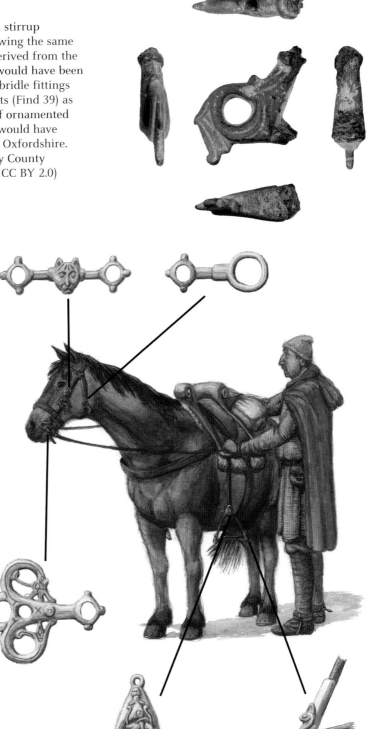

This small, hollow-cast, copper-alloy object is in the form of a square church tower of late Anglo-Saxon date and decorated in a manner comparable to the Winchester style. The side panels are openwork and depict angels with small central bosses alternating with panels that depict a flower bud between a pair of facing scrolls. There is a plinth at the base with two projecting rounded perforated lugs, and four lozengiform roof facets decorated with foliate motifs. The top of the object has a rounded terminal knop and there are eight smaller decorative knops at the angles between the roof panels.

Larger versions of this type of object have been identified as decorative covers for censers, designed to allow scented smoke to be emitted during church services. This is, however, difficult to prove directly, as they may just as easily be components for another type of church fixture such as lamps. This particular example, due to its small size, is better regarded as being an associated decorative fitting or mount, as it is difficult to see how it could function as something like a censer cover on its own. Whatever its function, it survives as a little insight into late Saxon church services. It is also incredibly rare, with only a few comparable examples known. The find has now been acquired by Guildford Museum.

Above left: A late Anglo-Saxon censer mount or liturgical fitting, AD 900–1100, Surrey. (SUR-777720, © Surrey County Council licensed under CC BY 2.0)

Above right: Another example recorded by the PAS; this one has been infilled with lead, apparently for subsequent use as a weight, Norfolk. (NMS-DFB8F0, © Norfolk County Council licensed under CC BY-SA 4.0)

This copper-alloy object has an openwork triangular plate with a central hole flanked by moulded animal heads. There is a zoomorphic decorated knop at the apex in the shape of an animal's head, with pointed oval eyes, a snout, a rounded brow and open jaws, which hold a rounded loop. At the other end of the plate are a pair of projecting loops.

Despite superficial similarities to buckles and stirrup-strap mounts, this object has a different function. It appears similar to later medieval hinged clasps, which were designed to hold book covers together to prevent the springy vellum pages popping the book open, risking damaging or soiling the pages within. The projecting loops would have held a hinge bar connected to a plate or strap attached to one cover of the book; the central hole would have then fitted over a peg on the other cover of the book, and the terminal loop would hold a ring or cord to assist in pulling the clasp from the peg. The bent terminal of this object could even be the result of an owner pulling too hard at the clasp to free it from the peg.

While such book clasps are not uncommon finds from later periods, in the eleventh century AD they are rare objects. Books were expensive handmade prestige items during this period and would not have been accessible to many people, aside from the clergy and nobility to whom they were treasured items that displayed the owner's wealth and status.

A book clasp, AD 1000–1100, from West Sussex. (SUSS-5AF9E0, © Sussex Archaeological Society licensed under CC BY-SA 4.0)

The reliance on a bullion economy by the Vikings has already been noted earlier (Find 37) and so it should not be surprising that this period also provides evidence for weights and measures. Indeed, it is in this period that we begin to see the first widespread identifiable evidence for such objects since the Roman period. This twenty-sided object weighs 14.58 g (½ oz) and was likely used as a bullion weight to conduct transactions using hacksilver.

It has ring-and-dot decoration on each of the eighteen pentagonal facets around the sides. The larger hexagonal facets on each side appear to have stamped inscriptions, one that is unclear but may be an arabic word reading أَمَن or 'Iman'. This also literally translates as 'faith' or 'belief', which may allude to the trustworthiness of the weight.

Polyhedral weights are a distinctive form known from the Danelaw and have frequently been suggested as mimicking those of the Eastern and Islamic worlds encountered in long-distance trade. This example may, however, have a more exotic origin, with comparable examples known from Turkey which have similar markings and stamps. It was probably such weights from the Islamic world that influenced the production of the more distinctly 'Viking' weights of the Danelaw.

A bullion weight, AD 900–1200, from Kent. (PUBLIC-009751, © Kent County Council licensed under CC BY 2.0)

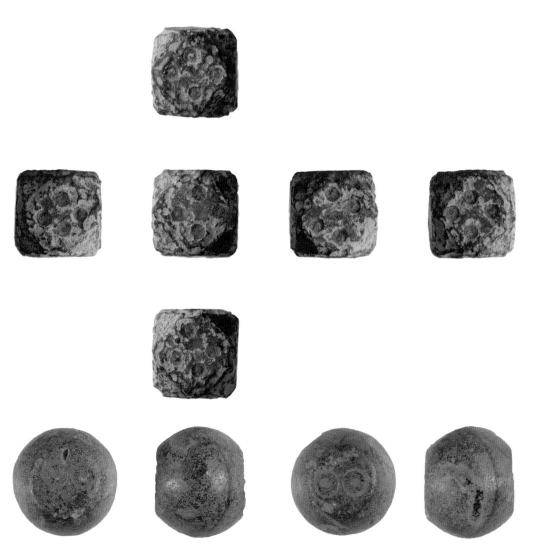

A polyhedral ⅛-oz bullion weight from Norfolk (NMS-A599E8, © Norfolk County Council licensed under CC BY-SA 4.0) and a distinctive ¼-oz barrel-shaped bullion weight, AD 820–1066, Lincolnshire (LIN-D449AC, © Lincolnshire County Council licensed under CC BY 2.0). The number of dots on each face likely indicates the unit value.

Chapter 5
Legacy and New Lords: The Later Eleventh Century AD

The return of Anglo-Saxon kingship under Edward the Confessor and Harold II was short-lived, with the later eleventh century becoming synonymous with the brutal invasion by William of Normandy in October 1066. This dramatic event rapidly saw the entire ruling class of England supplanted by a new type of overlord: the Norman Knight. For ordinary people, profound changes to the economy and land–ownership structures were to follow, with many being caught up in a restrictive feudal system somewhat different to their traditional ways of life.

The impact of this on Wales was somewhat more marginal, with local rulers able to persist into the middle of the Medieval period. This was brought to an end with the eventual expansion of Norman military control and castles into Wales, which had already stamped its authority onto the landscape of England.

In England, however, the persistence of well-established Saxon and Danish language and customs resulted in a stratified society where the rulers and the ordinary people spoke

A coin of Harold II, the last Anglo-Saxon king, dating to AD 1066. From North Lincolnshire. (NLM-D99091, © North Lincolnshire Museum licensed under CC BY-SA 4.0)

An illustration from a twelfth-century font fragment from St Bridget, Bridekirk, Cumberland. It has been described as having 'a strange mix of old Norse and old English script'. The decoration is very Romanesque but with hints of older styles such as the pellet central lines to some of the striking vinework. The inscription is rhyming and follows a typical Anglo-Saxon epigraphic tradition, roughly translating as 'Richard, he me wrought, and to this beauty carefully me brought'. (CO-0 1884. George Stephens, *Handbook of the old-northern runic monuments of Scandinavia and England*)

entirely different languages. For many years, this process was seen as rapid, with the Normans thought to have swept away many of the Anglo-Saxon cultural norms by the turn of the eleventh and twelfth centuries. However, an increasing body of evidence, particularly from finds recorded by the PAS, shows that many Anglo-Saxon and Scandinavian styles and traditions persisted into the Medieval period.

This suggests that at many levels of society the cultural change was not as absolute as was previously supposed. This may help explain why the material culture of the succeeding twelfth century has often seemed so sparse: it is possible that many of the objects previously assumed to be from the eleventh century due to their pre-Conquest style, are in fact from much later and have remained in use much further into the twelfth century than has previously been realised.

As many of the previous finds have shown, the Early Medieval period has long been divided (in art historical terms) into a sequence of Germanic and Scandinavian art styles, which follow on from and partially overlap each other chronologically. These help us date artefacts from the period when there is no other contextual information to go on. During the mid to late eleventh century, the final Anglo-Scandinavian art style to become prevalent was the Urnes style, with its characteristic fine tendrils looping around sinuous animal forms. In England, this was expressed on insular and native objects such as this finely made strap fitting.

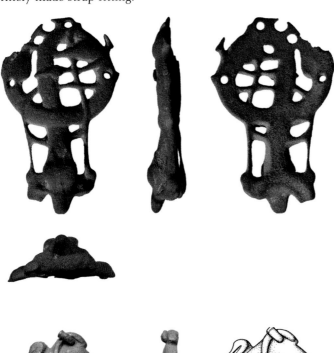

A strap fitting in English Urnes style, AD 1000–1100, West Sussex. (SUR-BFA968, © Surrey County Council licensed under CC BY 2.0)

A strap mount in English Urnes style, AD 1000–1100, Suffolk. (SF-69437C, © Suffolk County Council licensed under CC BY 2.0)

The precise function of this object is uncertain; it has an incomplete loop at one end which may have hooked to another fitting, and a broad openwork plate which was likely riveted to a strap. Its dominant feature is the curved animal which loops around the openwork plate, with the snout forming a terminal to the object and biting the incomplete loop at the end. The animal's body is surrounded by fine openwork tendrils which connect and frame the animal, typical of the Urnes style.

This object joins a growing corpus of mounts, strap fittings and a few brooches known in this style, which persists into the early twelfth century only to be finally eclipsed by new Continental traditions from France. These objects, perhaps, represent the final manifestation of the dominance of the Scandinavian cultural world on the dress and fashions of the people of Early Medieval England. In the western and northern fringes of Britain, however, particularly Scotland, this influence would persist for centuries yet to come.

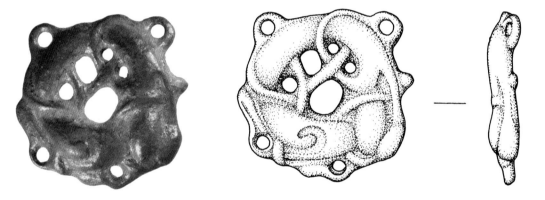

A smaller and simpler example of an object in the same style, Suffolk. (SF-6A969C, © Suffolk County Council licensed under CC BY 2.0)

As we have seen previously (see Find 25 and 26), objects with inscriptions can be some of the most personal and emotive of all, naming individuals or displaying religious devotion, as seen with this lead spindle whorl. This object had a vital function in increasing and maintaining the speed of the spindle when spinning wool. They are often considered very personal objects, with inscribed examples dating back to at least the eighth century AD and continuing to be seen into the medieval period.

Around its sides and base is a Norse runic inscription roughly reading, when translated, 'Odin and Heimdall and Þjálfa, they/ help thee Úlfljótr (a man's name) *kiriuesf*'. It clearly names the Norse gods Odin, Heimdall and the servant of Thor, Þjálfa. Unfortunately, the last and rather crudely inscribed word *kiriuesf* has yet to be deciphered. The runic lettering itself points to an eleventh-century date with the forms of the lettering, a dotted e-rune and shape of the o-rune being particularly indicative of the period. This dating is supported by the form of the spindle whorl which, while mostly being common from the sixth to tenth centuries, occurs at some urban centres, such as York, into the eleventh century. This striking, obviously pagan inscription is a fascinating piece of evidence for the survival of pagan religious belief, in a mundane and simple personal petition for blessing to the traditional powers of old.

Lead spindle with runic inscription from Lincolnshire. (LIN-D92A22, © Lincolnshire County Council licensed under CC BY 4.0)

A lead spindle whorl of twelfth-to-thirteenth-century date with a Middle English inscription but using an Old English epigraphic style naming the maker of the object. In this case: [R] Y C M : A D [:] þ A : W B E or 'Richard made thou be'. Updated translation suggested by the author. (LANCUM-DB9DC5, © The Portable Antiquities Scheme licensed under CC BY 4.0)

With the ever-growing power of the Church, ecclesiastical objects become increasingly visible as stray finds, although often not recognised as such historically. This object is a terminal or head piece, most likely from an ecclesiastical staff or sceptre, and one of a group of such objects now recognised as dating to the eleventh to twelfth centuries. Its design comprises an openwork cross with smaller diagonal arms between the main arms. This creates a wheel shape with open space between interconnecting lines highlighted by small pellets around the outer border and a central boss. The use of open space, borders of pellets or circles often combined with cross shapes is seen on many contemporary objects. These range from small lead disc brooches of the tenth to eleventh centuries, some notable early harness pendants and a relatively rare type of scabbard chape of the eleventh and twelfth centuries. The latter perhaps helps explain why these sceptre heads were initially misidentified as sword pommels.

Copper-alloy staff terminal from the Isle of Wight. (IOW-6995CD, © The Portable Antiquities Scheme licensed under CC BY 2.0)

The identification of these objects was helped by numerous excavated examples in secure contexts and increasing numbers of metal-detecting finds in the latter half of the twentieth century; including a number from the environs of churches or ecclesiastical institutions such as at Wixford in Warwickshire. Some later depictions, such as that of Edward the Confessor at Nayland's Church, Suffolk, show important figures carrying a sceptre or staff with a terminal at both ends. This suggests the possibility of a paired set, one at each end of the staff. There is some evidence for this, again from Warwickshire, as another, albeit spherical, terminal shows significant wear on the end opposite the socket. This indicates consistent use, perhaps with repeated contact with the ground. This also provides evidence for possible traditions of early church ritual surviving well into the later medieval period.

A lead brooch of nummular type showing bosses and borders of pellets coupled with a cross. (SF-AE4D73, © Suffolk County Council, licensed under CC BY 2.0)

47. An inscribed knife bolster and blade backplate, AD 1050–1200, Suffolk (SF-B8C2DC)
Dimensions: 113.45 mm × 21.08 mm × 11.07 mm

Knives are relatively scarce finds to be reported to the PAS from metal-detecting, as they are generally constructed from iron with organic handles, both of which survive poorly. Examples from the Early Medieval period are particularly rare, as most lack the copper hilt and handle-cap elements seen in later periods which are relatively common. A small group of late eleventh- to twelfth-century examples have been recently identified and are particularly notable, having both an end-cap (to help secure the handle), a bolster (a collar dividing handle and blade) and a decorative backing plate to the blade. In some cases, the plate and bolster are cast as one piece, as this example here. Astonishingly the two fragments were recovered by the same finder over a period of time.

The first of these knives (a complete example) was discovered at Waterford, Ireland, and, barring one fragment of a blade with a similar blade backplate, it was thought to be unique. In recent years, more examples like this one have come to light, with similar hexagonal bolsters/end-caps, often with inscriptions. This example includes an inscription running around the bolster and along each side of the plate. Although it is relatively clear, its full meaning isn't known; one side appears to directly reference the knife's use with part of the phrase translating as 'whoever cuts with a knife'. The Waterford example also makes reference to cutting, but as part of a religious blessing.

While the exact use and date of these knives is not clear, their ornate nature seems to mark them out in the period. The lettering seems to point to a late eleventh- to twelfth-century date and some other fragments make use of overtly Anglo-Saxon-style epigraphic formatting; by which the knife speaks directly to the reader, usually referencing who made it. The Waterford

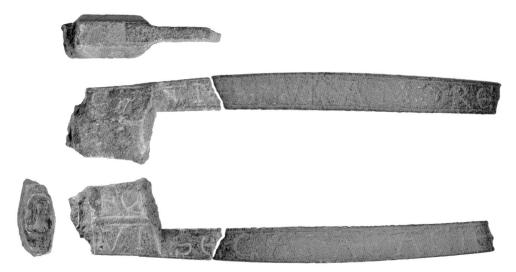

Copper-alloy knife fittings from Suffolk. (SF-B8C2DC, © Suffolk County Council licensed under CC BY 2.0)

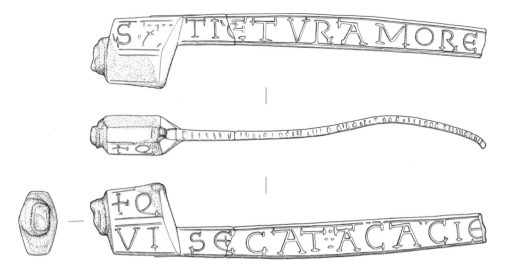

Illustration of how the knife fittings go together and clear representation of the inscription. (SF-B8C2DC, © Suffolk County Council licensed under CC BY 4.0)

An end-cap from another inscribed knife of this type with the beginning of the Anglo-Saxon epigraphic inscription 'ME FECIT' or 'made me'. (LIN-7E47B0, © The Portable Antiquities Scheme licensed under CC BY 2.0)

example, and perhaps this example, are inscribed with mottos combining cutting and religious references which may point to their use in religious ceremonies such as the cutting of bread for the Eucharist. This interpretation is supported by a twelfth-century knife with a religious inscription, albeit on a bone handle, which dedicates it to Notre-Dame, Paris.

48. A fragment sandstone ewer in Romanesque style, AD 1000–1200, Berkshire (BERK-CF5653)
Dimensions: 78.78 mm × 71.49 mm × 15.72 mm

Stone objects of Early Medieval date are unusual and rarely reported to the PAS. The few that have been are usually chance finds made while walking, gardening or undertaking agricultural work. This example was spotted by a diligent finder while out metal-detecting. Carved from a gritty sandstone, it is likely a fragment of miniature or portable stoup, or piscina, for holy water or other ritual cleansing. Around the outer face are saintly figures or perhaps Apostles within niches topped by rounded arches on distinctive columns.

The rounded arches and columns are distinctive of the Romanesque style, which was popular across western Europe and developed under the influence of both Roman, Byzantine and wider art and architecture of the Mediterranean. While often associated with monumental stonework, it does occur on metalwork and extends to zoomorphic designs as well. The rounded arch is very distinctive compared with the pointed Gothic arch that dominates later medieval buildings. While the style is often associated with the Normans, it made its way to Britain before the conquest. The long faces, wide eyes and style of the facial hair seen on this carving are very reminiscent of figurative depictions of the latter tenth and early eleventh centuries and may point to insular influence on the development of the style.

Carved sandstone stoup fragment. (BERK-CF5653 © West Berkshire licensed under CC BY 4.0, enhanced by the author)

Birds have been a popular motif on metalwork circulating in Britain since at least the Roman period, if not earlier. During the Early Medieval period, bird elements are common from some of the earliest zoomorphic designs. Various types of bird brooches exist, some being shaped like the bird itself and others, like this example, decorating the field of a disc or similar. Over time, these birds seem to become less the birds of prey of the earlier period, and more Christianised, with crosses on display. The bulbous bodies of these later examples and the use of Christian imagery usually suggest that the bird represented is a dove.

This brooch doesn't feature a cross, as seen on some of the earliest examples, but instead shows the bird holding a vine or branch in its beak. This could be a reference to the biblical dove of peace, depicted with an olive branch. However, this bird has a distinctly curved and predatory beak, and may suggest a more complicated evolution in bird representation. Birds and beasts with tendrils in their mouths had, by the time of this brooch's production in the eleventh or twelfth centuries, been used in decorative art for more than half a millennium, displaying a range of Christian and pagan influences. Birds were also a popular image in the Roman period, as is seen on a statue of an eagle devouring or fighting a snake recently found in London. This motif then persists on the early pennies (*sceatta*) of the seventh century AD, with various permutations demonstrating a continuity, however sporadic, of this classical iconography.

Enamelled bird brooch from North Yorkshire. (DUR-711E68, © Durham County Council licensed under CC BY 2.0)

An early penny (*sceat*) showing a bird, facing left, AD 720–740, Yorkshire. (NLM-6576B0, © North Lincolnshire Museum licensed under CC BY 2.0)

Different forms of bird brooch. An example with Scandinavian (Ringerike style) influences, AD 1000–1100, Lincolnshire (LIN-39FB8D © Lincolnshire County Council licensed under CC BY 2.0) and a cross-on-bird type, Hampshire (SUR-F46DF7 © Surrey County Council licensed under CC BY 2.0).

What complicates the identification and interpretation of this object is that it doesn't quite fit with the early group of enamelled Anglo-Saxon brooches of the ninth century. Enamelled metalwork had a resurgence in the twelfth century, often using similar bird with vine motifs, however, brooches like this are not generally seen to be in regular use at the time. As a result, there are potential difficulties of assigning this brooch, and its small associated group, a narrow date due to these discrepancies in form and iconography.

93

50. Gaping mouth buckle, AD 1000–1150, Kent (PUBLIC-EC2A87)
Dimensions: 35 mm × 14.66 mm × 18.9 mm

Gaping mouth buckles are a striking type of zoomorphic object, mostly dating to the twelfth century and made in the Romanesque style, seen by some as a distinctly Norman innovation. This particular example was the first to indicate this may not be the case and, along with a small number of other early examples such as LIN-3D61B5 from Lincolnshire, appears to demonstrate an Early Medieval origin for the type. Looking distinctly Anglo-Scandinavian and eleventh century in style with tendrils around the mouth and large eyebrows, this buckle anticipates the form of the later-twelfth-century type. The relative rarity of these early examples suggests that gaping mouth buckles did not gain wider popularity until the twelfth century.

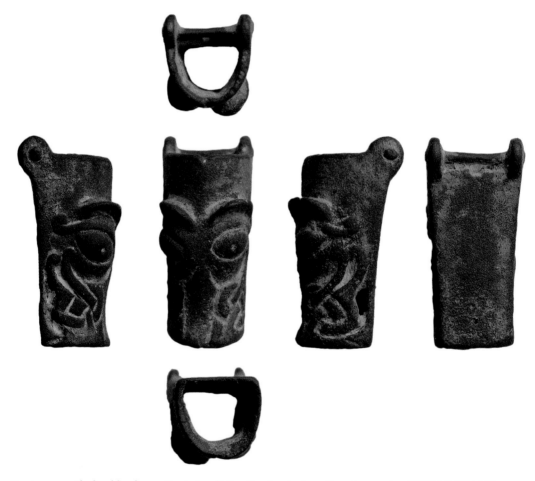

Gaping mouth buckle from Kent in distinctly Anglo-Scandinavian style. (PUBLIC-EC2A87, © Kent County Council licensed under CC BY 2.0)

Two gaping mouth buckles. *Left*: from Dorset, this is typical of the twelfth-century type. Its Romanesque design is evident in its squat face and pointy ears, typical of predatory animals depicted in the style (PAS-72DFB6, © The Portable Antiquities Scheme licensed under CC BY 2.0). *Right*: a gaping mouth buckle sharing the Romanesque style but with the distinctly thirteen-century offset strap bar common on simpler buckles of the time. (SF-E1A115, © Suffolk County Council licensed under CC BY 2.0)

What distinguishes these objects, compared with other finds discussed in this chapter, is their apparent longevity of use, with some examples appearing to persist into the thirteenth century. This is perhaps most clearly seen on SF-E1A115, which has an offset strap bar commonly seen on medieval buckles, a design immediately recognisable to many archaeologists and detectorists alike.

The transition in stylistic influences from Scandinavian to French seen in this particular group of objects in many ways encapsulates the very end of the Early Medieval period. It represents the transition of England from a North Sea kingdom tenuously holding on to independence from Scandinavian overlordship into a European power increasingly entwined in the politics of wider medieval Christendom.

Acknowledgements

Thanks are due to all the finders, metal detectorists, mudlarks, field walkers and beach combers who record their finds and enable this knowledge about the past to be preserved. Thanks also to the hard-working FLOs, FLAs and volunteer recorders whose work makes this book possible and the expert advisors including Kevin Leahy, Helen Geake, Elisabeth Okasha, John Hines, Sue Brunning and Gabor Thomas who help us to get the identifications correct. Thank you to all the museums staff who have shared images with us, including Dr Mike Still of Dartford Borough Museum, Amal Khreisheh of South-West Heritage Trust, Nadine Lees of Birmingham Museums Trust and to all the various artists whose drawings and photos are included; Eric Jones, Mark Gridley, James Cope, Andrew Williams, Andy Chopping (MOLA), Faith Vardy (MOLA), Elaine Butler (Regia Anglorum), Dominic Andrews, Lloyd Bosworth and all those unnamed others whose work has gone into producing the images illustrating the PAS records used in this book. Appreciation is also extended to Phil Moore for image editing advice and support. Thank you also to Imogen Harris for initial editing and proofreading prior to draft submission. Unless stated, all other images are courtesy of the Portable Antiquities Scheme and used under a Creative Commons (CC) licence.